Domains is published bi-annually in the United States by South Focus Press (244 Fifth Avenue, Suite 2802, New York, New York 10001, www.southfocuspress.org) under the editorial direction of Pradeep Jeganathan at the International Centre for Ethnic Studies, Colombo, Sri Lanka.

Domains is a refereed journal.

Domains One and other subsequent issues are available as books (ISBN: 0974883921, for this issue) through out the world, distributed by Ingram Book Company and Baker & Taylor in the US, Whitakers in the UK, and Ingram International in the rest of the world. These issues may be ordered from any bookstore in those countries, and is also available from amazon.com.

Domains is also available as a serial (ISSN: 1391-9768) through out the world. Subscribers in the United States, United Kingdom and Europe may purchase yearly subscriptions from www.southfocuspress.org: Institutions US$ 85.00, individuals: US$ 35.00.
Subscribers in Sri Lanka, South Asia and the global South may write to: The Librarian, Subscriptions, International Centre for Ethnic Studies, 2 Kynsey Terrace, Colombo 8, Sri Lanka for reduced rates.

Domains welcomes submissions of between 7,500-10,000 words, from all disciplines of the social sciences and humanities, pertaining to any geographical area of the world. Both purely theoretical and empirically rich articles are valued, if original and rigorously argued; thematically important are problems of subordinate and dominant nationalisms in post-colonial spaces, questions of statehood, rule and governance, conflict resolution and constitutional reform on the one hand and gendered violence and social suffering, cultural diversity and communal co-existence on the other. Domains is particularly interested in post-disciplinary intellectual projects such as postcolonial feminism, critical legal studies and subaltern studies. Submissions, which should include an abstract of 150-300 words, should be sent as a MS-Word attachment to submissions@icesdomains.org. For the most current information about special issues and themes visit www.icesdomains.org.

Printed in the United States of America, on acid free paper.

DOMAINS

Editor
Pradeep Jeganathan
International Centre for Ethnic Studies

DOMAINS

Number One, 2004

•

Dutiful Daughters, Sacrificing Sons: female-headed households in
Eastern Sri Lanka
Kanchana Ruwanpura
8

•

The Unconscious of Democracy: ideological hegemony and
nationalism in post-socialist Croatia
Ozren Pupovac
38

•

Desecularizing Secularism: Post-secular history, non-juridical
justice, & active forgetting
Ananda Abeyesekere
71

•

DOMAINS RECOLLECTS:
◦

Said, the European Novel & Imperialism: A critique
Regi Siriwardena
121

•

Dutiful Daughters, Sacrificing Sons: Female-Headed Households in Eastern Sri Lanka[1,2]

Kanchana N. Ruwanpura

ABSTRACT:
This article is a qualitative analysis of the ways in which female-headed households in eastern Sri Lanka use children to maintain the welfare of their families. When I began my fieldwork in eastern Sri Lanka (1998-99) one of my working hypotheses reflected the limited belief that girls in female-headed households were more likely to witness interruption to their education because of the conflict. During my fieldwork, however, I quickly came to realize that it is usually the oldest child, irrespective of gender, who would see her or his education disrupted. There were ethnic differences to the decisions made by female-heads. My point in this paper, however, is not to argue that decisions with respect to children's welfare are based simply on ethnic differences. Rather it is to draw attention to the complexities of the decision-making processes of female-heads and see them influenced and shaped by a convergence of conflict, material, cultural and patriarchal dynamics. A feminist analysis should move beyond the simplistic anticipation that the welfare of girls is likely to suffer in comparison with their brothers, and we need to complicate the frequently repeated simple story of gender bias. Ironically, boys should be seen to bear the brunt of patriarchy too.

1. The "Value" of Children

Children are an important resource for poor households and especially so for female-headed households[3]. The literature on

---

[1] This paper is a modified version of a chapter of my Ph.D dissertation: *Matrilineal Communities, Patriarchal Realities: Female-Headship in Eastern Sri Lanka — A Feminist Economic Reading.*

[2] The title of this article is motivated by a similarly titled paper "Moral Mothers and Stalwart Sons" by Malathi de Alwis and Simone de Beauvoir's *Memoirs of a Dutiful Daughter.*

[3] Following comprehensive typology developed by Nadia Youssef and Carol B Hetler, (*Women-Headed Household and Rural Poverty: What do we know?* (Washington, D.C.: International Center for Research on Women, 1981)), this

female-headship not only notes the economic importance of children for these households, but also observes the particular susceptibility of girls to early working and economic demands.[4] Unequal gender relations place less social and economic value on the human capital of girls, leading to the rapid deterioration of their capabilities. The implicit assumption here is that this is due to patriarchal structures that discriminate against girls and result in their removal from education.

It is true that inequities in gender relations entail girls and boys having different socio-economic values placed on them, and that these are perpetuated through cultural, patriarchal, material and religious structures. While the interactions of these institutions usually result in girls being relatively disadvantaged, the decisions that female-heads make are layered and complex. During my fieldwork,[5] done in 1998-99 in eastern Sri Lanka, it became apparent that children were indeed important in the female-headed households I surveyed across Muslim, Sinhala, and Tamil ethnic groups in eastern Sri Lanka[6]. Yet, there was a need for a more nuanced analysis, one which recognized that female-heads make difficult choices about which children should work, and that they provided different rationales for disrupting their daughters or sons education.

---

paper distinguishes between de facto and de jure female-headed households. De jure female headship occurs when women are pushed into assuming headship because of death, divorce, or legal separation from their male partner. The temporary absence of a male breadwinner and head because of migration, desertion, conflict-led abandonment, alcoholism, physical disability, underemployment or unemployment leads to de facto female headship. See Mayra Buvinic, Nadia Youssef and Barbara Von Elm, *Women-Headed Households: The Ignored Factor in Development Planning* (Washington, D.C.: International Center for Research on Women, 1978), 6.

[4] For more on this see Pradeep Kumar Panda, "Female Headship, Poverty and Child Welfare: A Study of Rural Orissa, India," *Working Paper no. 280* (Thirunanthapuram: Center for Development Studies, 1997).

[5] Appendix A at end of paper provides a brief summary of the fieldwork and research methodology that formed the basis of this study.

[6] Kanchana Ruwanpura, *Matrilineal Communities, Patriarchal Realities: Female-Headship in eastern Sri Lanka — A Feminist Economic Reading* (Ph.D diss., University of Cambridge, 2001).

When I began my fieldwork in eastern Sri Lanka my working hypothesis reflected the limited belief that girls in female-headed household were more likely to witness interruption to their education. During my fieldwork, however, I quickly came to realize that it is usually the oldest child, irrespective of gender, who would see her or his education disrupted. Recognizing this particular issue made me investigate further and engage with female-heads on the motives for taking boys out of school, where this occurred, rather than girls. My previous work shows that there was, however, an ethnic aspect to the decisions made by female-heads (Ibid). Normally, Muslim female-heads did conform to "convention" by taking girls out of school at an early age to help with domestic chores and/or self-employment activities, but this was less true for the Sinhala and Tamil communities. My point in this paper is not to argue that decisions with respect to children's well being are based simply on ethnic differences. Rather it is to draw attention to the complexities of the decision-making processes of female-heads and see them influenced and shaped by a convergence of material, cultural and patriarchal dynamics.[7] A feminist analysis should move beyond the simplistic anticipation that the welfare of girls is likely to suffer in comparison with their brothers, and we need to complicate the frequently repeated simple story of gender bias. Ironically, boys should be seen to bear the brunt of patriarchy too.

Using case studies of female-heads in eastern Sri Lanka, the complexities of human capital investment decisions regarding boys and girls are examined in this paper. Cultural, religious, social, and political norms color decisions made by female-heads. These decisions are not based only on economic considerations.

---

[7] In this respect my work is also distinct from the psycho-social literature on survival and trauma in eastern Sri Lanka done by scholars like Selvy Thiruchandran, *The Other Victims of War: Emergence of Female Headed Households in Eastern Sri Lanka: Volume II* (New Delhi: Vikas Publishing House, 1999). This research focuses on the ways in which female-heads have psychologically coped with death, destruction and displacement because of the ethnic and armed conflict in the province. My broader work on the other hand is interested in looking at numerous factors — and not just the conflict — that has led to female-headship in the region, and therefore the intersection between material conditions and conflict in the livelihood strategies devised by these female-headed households.

The complication is that female heads provide very different rationales, influenced by patriarchal premises, for disrupting either their sons' or their daughters' education.[8] Accordingly, the next two sections — 2 and 3 — of this paper investigate female heads' narratives on whether to disrupt the education of their girls or boys. Section 4 studies the connections and dynamics linking motherhood, dutiful daughters and sacrificing sons.[9] Through the narratives of female-heads, this section brings together the potency of maternal ideology in the socio-economic decisions made by female-heads with respect to their daughters and sons.[10] Finally, the concluding section, 5, links the short-term and long-term consequences faced by girls and boys of not realizing their human capabilities, particularly in female-headed households. This is partially accomplished through the retold experiences of the female-heads' own unsettled childhood and adolescent years.[11]

2. Patriarchal Logic and "Girl-Power"?

---

[8] This investigation also leads to my feminist methodology work in my dissertation, which argues that social reality is embedded in structures that require analysis — even though the outcomes depend on context, they are interconnected and highly differentiated. For more on this see Tony Lawson, *Economics and Reality* (London and New York: Routledge, 1997), and "Feminism, Realism and Universalism," *Feminist Economics*, 5 no. 2 (1999): 25-59.

[9] My thanks to Dr. Jane Humphries for suggesting the idea, and specifically for encouraging me to incorporate this focus on children in my Ph.D.

[10] In pursuing this exercise, I make extensive use of studies on motherhood, politics and nationalism in Sri Lanka, that provide a valuable precursor to developing similar themes in the economics of female-headed households. For more on this see Malathi de Alwis, "Motherhood as a Space of Protest," in *Appropriating Gender: Women's Activism and Politicized Religion in South Asia*, eds. Patricia Jeffery and Amrita Basu (London and New York: Routledge, 1998), 185-201. Also see her "Moral Mothers and Stalwart Sons," in *The Women and War Reader*, eds. Lois Ann Lorentzen and Jennifer Turpin (New York and London: New York University Press, 1998), 254-7. But motherhood as a social construct has also been subject to critique by feminist anthropologists, who have attempted to show its historical and cultural specificity. See Henrietta L Moore, "Mothering and Social Responsibilities in a Cross-Cultural Perspective," in *Good Enough Mothering? Feminist Perspectives on Lone Motherhood*, ed. Elizabeth Bortolaia Silva (London: Routledge, 1996), 58-75.

[11] This, of course, begs the question whether emphasizing the short-run negative consequences for children as a social group helps set the stage for pressing policy planners to integrate gender-sensitive policy prescriptions.

A standard feminist theme is that girls suffer disproportionately from poverty. This issue has been subject to much research in the Sri Lankan context[12]. An associated assumption is that girls' education is disrupted to allow them to contribute to family labor and/or to perform domestic chores. But the decision to make girls do such work is not determined solely by poverty[13]. Anecdotal evidence about decision-making by female-heads reveals that there is no single line of reasoning that dominated when the capability bases of their children were at stake. Reflection on their own economic difficulties made them critically re-evaluate the prevailing options for their daughters. Interestingly, the same themes ran across the accounts by female-heads of all ethnic groups of the factors that figure in their decision-making. Here, I begin with a discussion of those female-heads with little or no education who made the decision to educate their daughters, despite the associated economic hardships, because they viewed education as a stepping stone towards improved welfare for their daughters as well as for the household.

> Neither me nor my husband had studied beyond primary education, but a primary aim I have is to educate my daughters. Even though I face economic difficulties I hope to continue their education. To disrupt their education would be to hinder their ability to achieve better things.
> *(Savithri, a 35-year old Tamil de facto female-head from Trincomalee, and mother of three children.)*

> My husband is terminally ill and has been so for the past few years. Even though he is in hospital at present, when he is less severely ill we have to bring him home. Since I am working full-time as an agricultural laborer I am at home only during limited hours and this implies that one of my three daughters has to attend to my husband's needs. However, I am resolute in my decision not to dis-

---

[12] Center for Women's Research (CENWOR), The Girl Child in Sri Lanka, Document Series no. 46. (Colombo: CENWOR and UNICEF, 1993).
[13] See Richard Anker, "Conceptual and Research Frameworks for the Economics of Child Labor and its Elimination," *Working Paper, ILO/International Program on the Elimination of Child Labor* (Geneva: ILO, 2000), 28.

rupt their education, because I know the limited opportunities I have in seeking wage employment are due to my own inadequate schooling. So I make sure that my daughters and I share all responsibilities in caring for my ill husband as well as the domestic chores. This way, I hope, my daughters will be able to succeed in their studies as well and be able to have a better future than I will.

*(Jameela, a 42-year old Muslim **de facto** female-head from Ampara, and a mother of three daughters).*

Even when my husband was alive, there was no dispute about educating our children. I myself did not study beyond grade 8, but in today's society not having educated daughters is only going to make their lives harder. I want to make my daughter's life better than mine and for this I have to ensure that her education is uninterrupted.

*(Ramani, a 38-year old Sinhala **de jure** female-head from Trincomalee, and a mother of two children — where the daughter is schooling while the son is the main income earner for the household).*

These women's limited education combined with their experiences of economic hardships colored the decisions they made to struggle to continue schooling their daughters. They also show an ability to link their economic vulnerability to their limited education, which while undoubtedly aggravated by the ethnic conflict would continue even in a more peaceful environment. Moreover, by asserting their autonomy they are recognizing changes and transformations taking place in Sri Lankan society that require better-educated women to grapple with the future challenges their daughters will encounter.[14] Denied opportunities themselves as a result of poverty, "tradition" and culture, these mothers had ardent aspirations for their daughters and were willing to provide for them to obtain skills. In my previous work, the work on Mus-

---

[14] Among lower-income female-heads there is an interesting generation gap appearing on the issue of educating girls. "Traditional" views on women's education are challenged by women who have themselves had limited education. This echoes Uma Narayan's point that "it is impossible to describe 'our traditional life' without seeing change as a constitutive element affecting transformations..." See Uma Narayan, *Dislocating Cultures: Identities, Traditions and Third World Feminism* (New York and London: Routledge, 1997), 26.

lims quoted the reaction of a female-head who, upon her husband's death, flouted his views on limiting education for their daughters.[15] Her outlook reveals the readiness of female-heads to contravene patriarchal authority when the immediate sources of authority are weakened or removed.[16]

However, there are other female heads that invoke patriarchal logic to explain their decisions to keep their daughters in school. This group argued that because their culture prohibited young girls and women from moving around in public places, it was a much more cogent decision to keep their daughters in school.[17] Female heads explained their decisions as a black-and-white choice: either to remove daughters from education or keep them in school, where the former allowed them to help in domestic chores and the latter implied limited movement between home and school. By allowing their daughters to remain in school, female-heads reasoned that they were controlling the movements of their daughters, which was important in communities that frowned upon unnecessary mobility in public spaces[18]. Such a cultural rationale was often provided by female-heads in the Muslim and Tamil communities, but was less frequently an explanation used by Sinhala female-heads.

> I have had a very troubled marriage and all of this of course has made me aware of the need to have an independent access to income. And one possible option open to women to achieve this is through education, and so I have insisted that my daughters be educated. But also

---

[15] Ruwanpura 2001, 41.

[16] Such ruptures disclose the fluidity of "tradition" and "culture", which should be seized upon by feminists to espouse necessary policies that are not only gender-sensitive but also come from within communities. Gender-sensitive development policies that evolve from this project are discussed in greater detail in my dissertation (Ruwanpura, 2001).

[17] This reasoning had an adverse consequence for boys, who were more likely to have their education interrupted. I shall discuss this issue in greater detail in the following section, and here I only draw the reader's attention to this related issue.

[18] Dennis McGilvray, "Households in Akkaraipattu: Dowry and Domestic Organization among Matrilineal Tamils and Moors of Sri Lanka," in *Society From the Inside Out: Anthropological Perspectives on the South Asian Household*, eds. J. N. Gray and D. J. Mearns (London: Sage Publications, 1989), 192-235.

Hindu culture is more conducive to keeping daughters in school rather than getting them to work at an early ge. Getting girls to work at an early age is difficult when mobility of young girls is frowned upon in my community. So I decided to keep my daughters in school and ensure their educational success.

(Vasukhi, a 44-year old Tamil de facto female-head from Batticaloa, and mother of 6 children).

In this day it does not make much sense to keep daughters at home, because having educated daughters can only benefit them, their husbands and their families. But also I do not need all my daughters to stay at home and help in domestic chores, and getting them educated is still adhering to cultural norms that permit restricted movements for women in my community. They just move between home and school, and of course even after getting their educational qualifications it is possible for them to find jobs like teaching, secretarial work, etc. These jobs do allow young women their own income, but do not *appear* to confront values.

(Zareena, a 52-year old Muslim de jure female-head from Batticaloa, and mother of 4 children).

These arguments represent either silent challenges to "authentic" cultural readings or female-heads' creative use of cultural norms to promote the education of their daughters. While female-heads explained their preference for educating daughters in terms of cultural imperatives, it is of course very possible that these female-heads were simply appropriating patriarchal logic to justify what they wanted to do, namely keep their daughters in school. As third-world feminists have rightly pointed out, "there are many ways, of inhabit[ing] nations and cultures critically and creatively", and the possibility of female-heads reading and mobilizing cultural norms differently should not be dismissed.[19] The critical point is that daughters can derive benefits from prolonged schooling because of the decisions made by their mothers.

As much as ideological structures affect female-heads so do their material realities, and hence there were female-heads that

---

[19] Narayan 1997: 33.

did have to disrupt their daughters' education for economic reasons. However, although such decisions were made, they were not simple resolutions and usually involved a convergence of negative factors. Poverty coupled with illness, the need for extra help in home-based income generating activities and/or domestic chores, motivated these female-heads to disrupt their daughters' education. The description by Lakshmi, a 41-year old Tamil *de jure* female head, of her agonizing decision best epitomizes the complexity of her decision to discontinue the education of her oldest child, who also happened to be a girl. Lakshmi married at 15 years and was thrust into headship at 24 years, when her husband died of a poisonous snakebite. She, however, did not interrupt her oldest daughter's education as soon as her husband died, and as she mentioned: *"I knew it would be difficult, but I had all good intentions of continuing my children's education."* However, three years after her husband's death Lakshmi had a motorbike accident, which required her hospitalization. During this time Lakhsmi's oldest daughter, Logi, started staying at home to look after her siblings. When Lakshmi was discharged from hospital, she made the difficult decision to retain this arrangement, realizing that Logi could help her with domestic chores as well as in self-employment activities. In retelling the variety of factors that led to her decision, Lakshmi kept emphasizing both regret and the difficult choices she faced at this juncture of her life. She stressed that it was not simply poverty that compelled her to make the decision to interrupt her daughter's education. Other female heads similarly identified many adverse factors as forcing regrettable decisions about female children's education.

The low value placed on their daughters' education entered the discussion only in exceptional circumstances. This particular justification for interrupting girls' education was so rare, that further inquiry among Sinhala and Tamil female-heads was undertaken. Female-heads acknowledged the difficulties educated daughters may still have in obtaining employment commensurate with their education, especially given the economic turmoil and protracted ethnic conflict. However, these female-heads were insistent that the particular economic conditions in eastern Sri

Lanka would pass, and that education can never be a wasted opportunity. As most female-heads from these communities put it:

> We do not have any guarantees that educating our daughters will make them even get jobs after obtaining the necessary qualifications. There are many educated young girls who do not get decent jobs even though they have been educated up to O/Levels and A/Levels, and it is especially difficult given the political and economic turmoil in the region. But things will change and when this happens being educated women will only mean that the possibility of a *bright* future remains an option for our daughters. Those of us, who did have to terminate the education of some of our daughters, will only feel remorse for making this decision. And while a variety of circumstances may have brought this about, for not one minute did we delude ourselves into thinking that this was the best decision from the point of view of our daughters' welfare.[20]
> (*Views of a group of Tamil and Sinhala female-heads from the area*)

An interesting divergence was the stance taken by some Muslim and older female-heads. They reasoned that there were limited benefits in educating daughters for a variety of reasons, rehearsing the range of negatives from the need to limit the movement of girls, to obeying the wishes of husbands, to difficulties associated with finding suitable employment. Each of these themes needs deliberation since they stress the numerous ways in which patriarchal interests impinge on the welfare of girls, and consequently on adult women. The primary issue that this group of female-heads mentioned involved the limits placed on girls moving in public, and how educating girls after they reached puberty would involve having the girls chaperoned by elderly/trustworthy adults and/or brothers. With intense pressure on the time and work of most female-heads, the additional burden of

---

[20] Such sentiments are not altogether surprising since there is free education right through to university. However, while education is state-funded, this still does not mitigate the education-related expenses that households have to bear, and in this respect such a strong emphasis on education perhaps indicate shifts in attitude towards education between different generations of female-heads.

escorting their daughters to school was not welcomed by many. Since exposing daughters to unguarded mobility in public spaces diminished their prospects of marriage and a better life, it was a serious threat not only to the family as a whole but also to the daughter. Educated girls who have moved freely in public spaces will have reduced their potential to marry eligible men, and having unmarried daughters is likely to create more economic and emotional stress for female-heads. So in a community where permissible marriage can only take place within the group, girls may be enhancing their capabilities at the cost of marriage. It is not girls getting an education per se which is at stake in these circumstances, but rather that this process involves other social sacrifices that need to be weighed by female-heads in the quest to make their daughters' lives better. The choices here are not easy ones. For these girls, it is either a better education with fewer marriage options, or apparently more marriage options and limited education.

Moreover, female heads reasoned that a better education might lead to unnecessary conflict with their potential spouses, who were anyway more interested in dowry[21] than in having educated wives. Educated women usually had opinions on issues, such as children's education, health, work patterns, etc., that might be incompatible with their husbands' views and lead to needless clashes. Furthermore, while education was free (i.e. state-provided) there were still incidental costs, such as books, uniforms, and transportation. Female-heads, noting the need to make savings for dowries and the possible negative implications of education for their daughters, had to weigh the constraints on their limited income when making decisions. A related issue was that

---

[21] This is an important social issue facing many young women from the middle-classes in the region — and especially Tamils, where the killings and/or migration of young men have put severe pressure on the supply of suitable boys to whom families could marry their daughters. It is reported that "eligible" men residing in foreign countries demand $50 000.00 dowries, which most households —and not just female-headed households— are unlikely be able to raise, leaving many young girls to be spinsters. (Source: BBC Report by Frances Harrison on "Bride and Groom" presented in the bbc.co.uk web page on South Asian issues, dated April 17th 2001).

even if they had educated their daughters and they had the necessary skills to find employment in the formal labor market, once married they were supposed to abide by the wishes of their husbands. Female-heads here, therefore, reasoned that there was no guarantee that their sons-in-law would permit their daughters to work once married, especially since the men would be risking their own social reputations by allowing their wives to work. These women continued to claim that it was not that they thought a working man's income would necessarily be sufficient to meet household expenses, but rather that when there was a need for women to augment household income, the work would have to be confined within the household. This group of female-heads would typically cite home-based income-generating activities as possible occupations. Married women would be likely to choose such activities because they supplement household income without upsetting the delicate balance of marital relations. So where older and Muslim female-heads encountered economic hardship and/or poverty, they argued that it was necessary to bear in mind other social issues when making decisions regarding their daughters' education. Consequently, there was a limited and/or low value placed on educating their daughters when they factored other considerations into the equation, and dutiful daughters did forfeit their personal welfare in such situations.

Significantly, however, there is a notable shift in attitudes of female-heads taking place that sometimes involved the tactical manipulation of patriarchal structures to protect the interests of their daughters. Female-heads here are clearly prudent in their politics. While they may not overtly challenge restrictive social and patriarchal structures, and mayseemingly may adhere to traditional ways, they are also guardedly expanding the spaces of social and economic opportunity for their daughters. Dutiful daughters may take on many guises. Some have their personal well-being promoted, while the welfare of others is more likely to be linked to their spouses. "Girl power", perhaps not, but certainly there are instances where female-heads turned the logic of patriarchy on its head to protect and promote the interest of daughters. As a Muslim female head aptly reminded me:

What is important in our community is that we *seem* to observe social norms. Cultures do not simply change. We have to make them change without disrupting existing social relations in one go. It is not an easy task, but it can be done. If men are increasingly unreliable then there should be no reason why we should not equip our daughters with more capabilities to overcome the hardship they may have to face. I always "listen" to my neighbors, relatives, and community but I make the final decision — and this is usually to ensure the current and future welfare of my daughters. On this, I will not fail them.
(Sameera, a 54-year old Muslim de jure female head from Ampara, and mother of three daughters).[22]

3. Patriarchal Structures that Stump the Boys

Earlier work highlighted the important economic support that sons provide to female-heads[23]. It was not simply girls who had to forgo improving their personal welfare and capability base. Support from sons is not limited to those who have been educated until the end of their secondary school and/or graduate education. Substantial proportions of sons have had their education disrupted at their father's desertion and/or death. Usually older sons, whether the eldest or not, were taken from school and expected to provide for the household. Female-heads of households across all communities used this route to replace the loss in income they encountered with the absence of their spouse. In rare instances it was a panic reaction by female-heads, but there was a crucial difference between the rationales given by female-heads in the differ-

---

[22] Readers, however, should be aware that female-heads' emphasis on educating their daughters is not necessarily consistent with other gender-conscious moves. Later I shall illustrate how improving children's welfare is usually done at the expense of female-heads' self-worth and well-being, and that this is because "good mothers" are willing to make many sacrifices to sustain the households welfare level. So the fervent adherence to maternal ideology contradictorily continues to perpetuate gender roles and norms through the social and patriarchal values female-heads inculcate in their daughters.

[23] See Kanchana Ruwanpura and Jane Humphries, "Female-Headship in eastern Sri Lanka: A Comparative Study of Ethnic Communities in the Context of Conflict," Working Paper No. 10, ILO-IFP/Crisis (Geneva: ILO, 2003); and their "Mundane Heroines: Conflict, Gender, Ethnicity, and Female-Headship in eastern Sri Lanka," Feminist Economics, 10, no. 2 (2004): 173-205.

ent communities, with Muslim female-heads emphasizing the ease of mobility of boys who therefore were suitable candidates for work from an early age. Sinhala and Tamil female-heads echoed each other in citing the wages sons were likely to muster, their physical ability to perform agricultural tasks, and security objectives, in that getting sons to work left them less likely to join the military and/or para-military forces.[24] Each of the motivations provided by female-heads, however, did entail sons, like their sisters in certain instances, having to make sacrifices in terms of their individual welfare and not having the opportunity to expand their capability base. They too, more often than not, had to give precedence to the interest of their family, especially where families were large, because "responsible" sons were expected to do so. Equally, Muslim and Tamil female-heads pointed that sons are valuable only when single. Upon marriage their responsibility shifts to their wives' families. Therefore, extracting the benefits

---

[24] An important distinction between the two communities, however, should be noted. For the Sinhala community, joining the military forces is increasingly becoming an effortless option, given the recruitment drives of the forces as well as the increasingly low educational requirements placed on lower-level military cadres. Joining the military forces, therefore, provides households with an assured monthly income, and even the high risks of being killed in the ethnic war is weighed against the monetary compensation that households receive from the State. Furthermore, de Alwis notes the ideological and gender images the State, via the media, deploys in calling on both mothers and sons to protect the nation-state. (See her "Moral Mothers and Stalwart Sons".) Some Sinhala female-heads, however, expressed ambivalence about their sons joining the military forces, mentioning that protecting their lives was more important than defending the country. While these Sinhala female-heads may be a critical and/or cynical few, their views were important in explaining the motivations for getting their sons to work and boosting household income from an early age. They explained that by getting their sons to work from an early age, they were instilling economic and social responsibility in them. And once this was so, they hoped that their sons joining military forces would be much less likely — and this was probably so, if only because they might not have the stipulated educational qualifications. For Tamil female-heads the threat of their sons being abducted by the L.T.T.E. as child soldiers is very real, and this took place frequently when boys were attending school. Where it was not forced abduction, boys were more likely to join the para-military forces voluntarily where men (their fathers) had been indiscriminately killed and/or tortured by the State military. Female-heads reasoned that by getting their sons to work, not only did they contribute to the household income, infusing them with social and economic responsibility, but also it became possible to keep an eye on their movements.

from sons needed to take place before they reached marriageable age. A Tamil female-head of household mentioned this in the following way:

> After marriage a son's responsibility is towards his wife and her family. Only a rare gem would still give precedence to his family — this happens, but is rare. So in the absence of a husband, I have to make sure that my sons do ensure the economic stability of the household, and especially of my daughters.[25]

In an attempt to depict the complexity of the social world of female-heads and their children, I discuss some main features that lead boys to stumble because of the different ways in which patriarchal structures operate.

Mobility is a male prerogative in the Muslim community, and seems to especially hold true for middle- and upper- income groups. While women in low-income groups may not have the luxury of being able to limit their activities to the household compound, they do attempt to adhere to the norms with their children, especially young, single and unmarried daughters. Where daughters have not been pulled out of school by Muslim female heads to help with domestic chores and/or self-employment activities, then it is boys who are likely to play an active role in supporting the household economically. Boys do not have restrictions on their mobility and this provides the primary grounds for removing them from school to participate in income-generating activities. These tasks ranged from finding wage employment, usually as casual laborers, to taking a prominent role in self-employment activities. Moreover, boys are better able to bargain, thus being a more adept link between household economic activities and the wider market. The use of boys as an essential support in self-employment activities indicates the burdens they faced in the community. Yet again, I quote the sentiments of a few Muslim

---

[25] Such views of female-heads and their relationship to their sons are undoubtedly linked to matrilineal norms, and are a predominant way of organizing kin structures in the region (McGilvray).

female-heads to explain the processes that can sometimes place boys in precarious positions.

> My main income comes from grounding and packaging flour for sale. The main thrust of the work involved I can do, but I have the choice of selling the packaged flour through a middleman, in which case I get a low price. Or I get my son to do the rounds in the town area, negotiate with shopkeepers and get a sound price. While I have studied up to grade 7 and I have the basic knowledge for engaging in such transactions, there are too many pressures on my life. When my husband died my 5 children were young, and I knew that I could not look after them, do self-employment work, and do the buying of raw material and selling the final product without any help. So I decided to get the oldest son involved by getting him to do the main buying and selling — but also getting his physical help in helping me with the tasks. Of course, this did mean disrupting his schooling even though he was 13 years then, but I feel I had little choice under the circumstances.
> (*Zahara, a 38-year old Muslim de jure female-head from Trincomalee, and mother of 5 children*).

> I had not studied beyond grade 5 and I had never been allowed to move in public spaces. I did have a very protected life as a young girl and then as a married woman. So when my husband died of a heart attack, I felt helpless. My eldest, my son, was 16 years and my youngest was then 8 years old. While a relative put me in touch with a N.G.O. that helped me set up a scheme of buying and selling short-eats, I still needed additional help in buying and selling the goods. I spoke with my older children, as I started treating them as equals, about all this, and we decided that my eldest son would stay back and work with me. So 10 years later, I have a fairly successful business and have managed to educate my other 7 children as well. We had tough times and hard decisions to make, but the worst is now over.
> (*Fathima, a 49-year old Muslim de jure female-head from Ampara and mother of 8 children*).

The inexperience of Muslim female-heads in their exposure to public interactions and/or their inability to move in public spaces to some extent determines the decision to interrupt their sons' education. Their own limited experience makes them hesitant to participate in activities that require asserting their will and making decisions, at least in public interactions. As a result they inevitably turn to their sons to get the necessary help and support, even if this implies taking their sons out of school. In fact many female-heads that had relied on young sons for economic support, considered this an obvious choice in a community where there was restricted movement for women and girls. So while girls were usually able to continue with their education in such situations, boys had to forgo the accumulation of human capital through education.

Boys are placed in insecure positions in female-headed households in the Sinhala and Tamil communities too, and since their mothers too typically expressed similar sentiments I now consider the core premise of their claims simultaneously. Where female-heads had access to land and were occupied in agricultural and/or home-gardening activities, they noted the need for physical labor in undertaking these tasks. In the absence of husbands to undertake these tasks, and without extensive support from male kin, mostly because there were fewer men in the area, female-heads decided to withdraw sons from schooling.[26]

> When my husband started leaving me for sporadic time periods, I rented some nearby land to begin cultivating vegetables for saleable purposes — and I was mostly doing this on my own. However, when I decided to separate from my husband permanently then I also spoke with my children and expressed the need for physical help to carry out the home gardening scheme profitably. Accordingly, I decided that my two older sons would support me with these tasks and the three of us now work together on the land

---

[26] In my dissertation I noted in the literature review chapter similar experiences by female-heads in South Asian and other countries, where there was lack of consistent support from male kin for agriculture-related tasks (Ruwanpura, 2001:12). In that case, however, it was explained by male kin recognizing that reciprocal help from female-headed households was unlikely and, therefore, limiting any help to such households.

This was the response of a Tamil *de facto* female-head. Similarly, other female-heads noted the ability of men, even young boys, to earn better wages by hiring themselves out as casual wage and/or agricultural laborers. They argued that by getting their sons to work from an early age, boys were able to acquire the necessary skill and training as future workers, and this was in addition to the important contribution they made towards the household income. While poverty thrusts some female-heads into reliance on their sons, they also argued that getting their sons to work from an early age is not necessarily negative.[27] Some female-heads did mention that these outcomes may not be the best for their sons, but their economic situation necessitated painful decisions. Finally, the political threat of their sons joining the military and/or para-military forces made female-heads remove them from school to work alongside them. In this way, most female-heads felt that they could monitor their sons' movements and activities, and any unnecessary association with others was kept at a minimum. The reality of the political conflict and ethnic war, therefore, enters into the decision-making process of female-heads — not only making their economic insecurity very real but also jeopardizing the chances of having a "normal" childhood for boys in the region. The key point is that not all boys benefit from patriarchal structures.[28] Some boys do have a price to pay, at least in the short run, and feminists should pay attention to these contradictions so as to comprehend the complexity of patriarchy itself.[29]

---

[27] When Anker discusses issues related to child labor, he makes a comparable point when he contends that "non-hazardous work might provide children some valuable life skills whereas idleness would not", in discussing the relationship between the quality of schooling and child labor (23).

[28] An interesting observation about the choices made by female-heads for their sons and daughters is the perpetuation of gender roles. The boys replace their fathers and the girls replace their mothers, allowing her to do work that her husband would normally have done.

[29] Additionally, recognizing the contradictions of patriarchal structures in relation to children helps further my feminist methodological argument that diverse outcomes are possible under patriarchy.

3.1 Maternal Ideology — Inter-linked Dynamics to Sacrificing Sons and Dutiful Daughters

Whose education faces disruption varies from household to household according to the circumstances and perceptions of female-heads. But not all female-heads made the choice to interrupt their children's education. Though children still remained an invaluable source of support in such households, since they performed tasks ranging from caring for siblings to marketing, there was a conscious decision to attempt to hang on to educating children and to delicately balance schooling with household activities. But the endeavors of female-heads to keep their children in school were in most instances linked to a strong maternal ideology that was articulated by these women. Female-heads were willing to forfeit their "good name" to provide their children with a decent and good upbringing, so maintaining particular patriarchal structures while challenging others. Here, female-heads were not sacrificing their sons' futures and not compelling their daughters to be duty-bound, they were generating an image of the mother who creates, nurtures and preserves life[30]. I contend that female-heads also sustain their families through personal sacrifices. Yet, by making personal sacrifices and even transgressing the acceptable boundaries of womanhood, these female-heads simultaneously, usually implicitly, subverted other patriarchal structures. Noting such contradictions is critical for feminists, since they may be used to counter seemingly stable patriarchal processes. Maintaining particular pillars of the status quo may sometimes require destabilizing other support structures, but where such paradoxes occurred without a conscious decision by female-heads then they were likely to reinforce a maternal ideology that did little to challenge gender and class hierarchies.

There were, however, other moments where female-heads made a conscious decision to challenge patriarchal norms on both womanhood and motherhood, thus asserting their agency and creating moments of possibility for evolving social transforma-

---

[30] For more see de Alwis, "Moral Mothers, Stalwart Sons," 188.

tions. I shall begin with a discussion, through anecdotal evidence, where challenging norms happened within the contours of propriety and consequently softened the nature of these challenges because it reinforced the concept of maternal ideology.

The decisions female-heads have to make are sensitive. They have to balance the welfare of the household and children against the perceptions of community and/or kin structures.[31] With kin and community support so critical for female-heads, putting families and children before themselves even to the point of threatening their own good name could potentially destroy the supportive network structures. Equally, it could undermine relationships with immediate kin that are critical for the households' welfare. However, some female-heads are willing to risk their personal welfare to promote the well being of the household, even though this may imply putting into peril their network base. Through the use of a particular case study I attempt to capture the dynamics of this process, where the female-head justified her actions by constantly harping on the rhetoric of motherhood — while her own mother was vociferously critical of the choices made by this female-head on the grounds of womanhood.

A female-head, her female-head daughter and other social relationships.

Kumari is a 41-year old Tamil de jure female-head in Ampara, whose husband was killed by the state in 1987. When her husband was alive she lived with him and her two daughters, where the elder was prone to severe epileptic fits from childhood. Since her husband's abduction and killing, her older daughter had had several recurrent epileptic fits that left her severely handicapped.

Around the same time Kumari's younger sister, who was in a bad marriage, was advised by their mother (Vijayai) to leave her

---

[31] I have developed an account of the relationship between community and kin structures, and its importance to female-headed households' well-being levels in my Ph.D work. It is sufficient to note here that this relationship is an important one, and is usually taken into account when female-heads make decisions regarding their households.

spouse, and this even though she was a mother of two sons. Kumari's older sister-in-law was expecting her first child but was to die in childbirth, leaving an infant in the care of her husband and his family. (This was occasioned by the prevailing conflict situation cutting off the links with her natal family, who was from Trincomalee). Vijayai made the decision to care for her granddaughter, acting as a surrogate mother. Since Kumari's husband was killed at the same time, the decision was made for both Kumari's sister and mother — with the young children — to move into Kumari's house.

While the three family units live in the same house, they do not share the same kitchen — which was the result of a series of disputes between Kumari and her mother. The tensions in the social relationships between Kumari and her mother epitomize the strength of maternal ideology and notions of "proper" womanhood that were expressed by the two women on separate occasions to me.

Kumari mentioned to me that as her husband had died, two of her siblings provided economic support — but she knew that it was not a permanent source of economic support. Therefore, she began tailoring clothes for people in the neighborhood — and branched out into several other sources of income generation, including poultry farming. During the time I met her she was undergoing a training session in carpentry — a non-traditional craft occupation for women — organized by a Canadian funded NGO. I was curious, therefore, to note Kumari's opinions on the choices that she made for herself to maintain the well being of her daughters. She mentioned that maintaining the welfare of her two daughters was her primary concern and she definitely did not want to disrupt her younger daughter's education — even though ensuring her older daughter's mental health placed both her and her younger daughter in a precarious situation. So drawing upon many avenues of income generation was an obvious choice, because "female-heads are vulnerable in the community, since we *have neither economic nor social security. And I am not even sure if female-heads working has brought a shift in attitudes towards us. But I do know that my daughters and their welfare are very important to me, and I will do anything to make their lives better — this even though I know that my own mother does not approve of me working with/through the NGO."*

Since Vijayai (a 59-year old) was also a female-head with whom I had extensive conversations, she did speak about the various economic and social issues she had to confront in bringing-up her granddaughter. She had particularly strong views on female-heads and the proper role of women, where she noted "People in the community are waiting for an opportunity to gossip about any wrong turn taken by my two daughters, since neither of them have husbands." Yet at the same time she was recounting various anecdotes of other female-heads that, in her view, were behaving improperly. It was during this dialogue that she mentioned her disapproval of Kumari's decision to take up the training course offered by the NGO. "She has a lamassi (teenage daughter) who has severe mental disabilities. Is it right that she leaves her daughter with us and goes out to work? Do 'good' mothers and women do such things?" she rhetorically asked me.

Juxtaposing conflicting views on motherhood and womanhood in this particular case study helps elucidate the inherent tensions between the various patriarchal concepts that female-heads use to shape their behavior. Younger female-heads were willing to challenge convention so that they could secure better opportunities for their children, and in doing so they justified their actions and behaviors within the rubric of motherhood. Thus, while they may be expanding the capability bases of their children, by sustaining their educational opportunities, their behavior is likely to inculcate in children patriarchal concepts of appropriate social roles. Aspiring to maternal roles does very little to subvert the accepted contours of gender relations: although female-heads may be increasingly accessing independent sources of income, a seeming challenge to the patriarchal *status quo*, they do so by resorting to another gendered standard, "motherhood", to validate their transgressions. Implicitly, through their own behavior and actions, most female-heads socialized their daughters and sons into the prevalent gender *status quo*.[33]

Thus, older female heads pointed to the "improper" behavior of younger female-heads when they undertook tasks that did not seem appropriate to their circumstances, were frequently seen in public, and/or were engaged in a multitude of self-employment schemes. The interesting twist in the intrinsic ambiguities of patriarchal structures came in those rare instances when female-heads made the necessary associations, and acted to assert their rights with a social awareness of these issues. The view of one Muslim female-head conveys this rare insight.

> I do not have people controlling my behavior and I do not listen to every utterance. This is because every aspect of our behavior is subject to some criticism or another. If we work, then this is questioned, and if I get our children to work then this is criticized too. I made the decision that my daughter should continue with her studies, because I think good schooling is the passport to a girl's success — she will be able to stand on her own two feet. But also I continue working and being active in the community, helping other vulnerable female-heads. If Chandrika, a widow, can be the President of Sri Lanka, then all other women can aspire to similar heights. It is usually patriarchal structures — which come in many forms and shapes — that prevent women from realizing their capabilities.
> (*Fasmeena, a 32-year old* **de facto** *Muslim female-head from Batticaloa, and mother of one daughter*).

Fasmeena was an exception in articulating the relationship between patriarchal structures, womanhood and mothering with such keen awareness. But it is important to note that there were other such women, though limited in number, and that these cut across the ethnic groups. They were conscious of the political, social and economic transformations taking place in the region, and made the connection to how their particular predicament was

---

[33] Additionally, those female-heads that choose home-based occupations both implicitly and explicitly reinforce notions of proper womanhood and motherhood simultaneously — and the high frequency of such events among female-heads across all ethnic communities is of course a cause for concern.

linked to the dynamics of this process. While their economic insecurity may have been compounded by their being thrust into assuming headship, and in most instances it was this that propelled
them to seek employment — whether as wage laborers, white-
collar workers and/or home-based workers — many of their other
decisions challenged patriarchal structures. And acknowledging
the multiple ways in which their lives were circumscribed by these
structures was the route adopted by such female-heads. This was
most visible on the question of their relationship with their children, where the decision to keep their daughters (and sons) in
school was made in conjunction with that of seeking employment,
thus reflecting their interests as well as those of the household.
Usually, such female-heads began their working-life as home-
based workers but through their own initiative made the effort to
obtain training in other crafts so that they were able to branch
out. Such female-heads recognized the importance of their own
well-being as well as that of their families, though at no time did
they perceive such an economic route as the only path to flouting
structures that usually placed restrictions on them. A young Sinhala *de facto* female-head aptly declared:

> I do not make enough money to consider myself wealthy
> and I barely live a comfortable life. However, one need
> not have money to interrogate structures that restrict our
> behavior. Yes, we need to be economically sufficient —
> because otherwise we do have to depend on kin and com-
> munity relations to a great extent, which may stifle our
> behavior. But my consciousness did not come about be-
> cause of stable employment. This helps, but before like
> many others I was primarily depending on homework,
> when I realized that this is an exploitative trade to be in
> — and since I had studied until my O/Levels I decided to
> volunteer part-time to a N.G.O. until I was permanently
> employed by them. With this exposure, each time a kin
> and/or community member said this was not right/proper,
> I began to challenge them — and ask myself — the rea-
> sons. Now I think what usually makes a good woman and
> mother is perception promoted by society, and what soci-
> ety says can always be changed.
> (*Swarna, a 27-year old Sinhala* **de facto** *female-head from
> Ampara, and mother of 2 children*).

Such sentiments reveal the willingness of some female-heads to act autonomously and question the various strands of patriarchal ideology, including maternal ideologies and notions of womanhood. These instances are not only inspiring for feminists, but also provided illustrations of the diverse ways in which female-heads may interpret similar experiences. But the general picture of female-heads is one infused by a strong notion of maternal ideology and womanhood, without the space for emancipation and/or realization of their social, political, and economic base.[34] Given this scenario, how then do maternal ideological constructions impinge upon daughters and sons who remain in school, as well as on those who get withdrawn from school? Does the former group necessarily end up having the potential to overcome the structures that make their mothers' lives vulnerable? Obviously, the response is contingent upon many factors, including their ability to make the necessary associations between different structures that preclude political, economic, and social security in most female-headed households. However, a more vulnerable group is that of girls who have had their education disrupted during their early years. They, I will argue in the next section, are more likely to suffer in the long term than boys with similar experiences of limited schooling. But I conclude by emphasizing the need to focus on the short-term negative consequences that children, as a group, are likely to suffer by having their education in-

---

[34] This is not altogether surprising. Other feminist scholars working on motherhood and womanhood in Sri Lanka have pointed to particular constructions of these concepts in nationalist projects — whether Sinhala or Tamil — that allow little space for creatively contesting patriarchal and class structures. See Sitralega Maunaguru, "Gendering Tamil Nationalism: The Construction of 'Woman' in Projects of Protest and Control," in *Unmaking the Nation: The Politics of Identity and History in Modern Sri Lanka*, eds. Pradeep Jeganathan and Qadri Ismail (Colombo: Social Scientist Association, 1995), 158-75; de Alwis in Jeganathan and Ismail, 1995; Qadri Ismail, "Constituting Nation, Contesting Nationalism: The Southern Tamil (Woman) and Separatist Tamil Nationalism in Sri Lanka," in *Subaltern Studies XI: Community, Gender, Violence*, eds. Partha Chatterjee and Pradeep Jeganathan (New Delhi: Permanent Black, 2000), 212-82. Unfortunately, however, similar anthropological and/or historical studies uncovering the relationship between gender and nationalism in the Muslim community have not been done.

terrupted. This is an important point for feminists in advocating development policy that is politically strategic.

3.2 Conclusion: Saving the Children?

Patriarchy is a complex set of social arrangements. However, feminists too often narrate a simple-minded story where patriarchy victimizes girls, especially in poor and female-headed households. By focusing on children and maternal ideology, I have shown the many varied ways in which patriarchal concepts and thoughts are used. Sometimes, female-heads creatively resorted to patriarchal justification to further the welfare of their daughters, often at a cost to their sons. Moreover, their decision to continue and/or disrupt the schooling of their sons and daughters was not simply and only linked to poverty. Poverty was an important variable, but where female-heads recognized the importance of educating daughters then they would justify their decisions by turning upside down the patriarchal logic that usually limits the education of girls. Female-heads' own experiences, coupled with economic exigencies, usually colored their decisions on educating daughters, while boys carry the economic burden. Where female-heads did take such actions, they ruptured patriarchal structures. This exposes the simple-mindedness of always seeing women and girls as victims and complicates decisions on children's schooling where female-heads are faced with bitter choices. However, by showing how such ruptures were the result of maternal ideology, I stressed the limitations and added caution to my optimism. Where decisions on children were linked to conventional ideas about maternal roles, any enthusiasm for the emancipation of female-heads must be tempered accordingly. Similarly, it is important to analyze in more detail the outcome in the long term for girls and boys who did have their education discontinued. Girls in this group are not simply thwarted from realizing their capabilities for ideological reasons but also may be unable to build upon their social capital base, whereas boys in similar situations only have to overcome a lower educational capability base. Ideologically and institutionally, the array of structures stacked against boys, as adults, will be of a lesser magnitude.

Female-heads' own experiences also influence decisions on their children's education in another important way. Mothers may resist disrupting either girls' or boys' schooling by behavior that compromises their reputation. But some female heads challenged such constraints to be good mothers by recognizing the patriarchal controls imposed through the ideology of the "good mother". Such female-heads were rare gems that challenge constraints because they are unjust, but nevertheless they effectively articulated the inequities embedded in gender relations by linking them to their own experiences as female-heads, mothers and women. Rajini, a 38-year old Tamil female-head, expressed her extraordinary insight on these issues as follows:

> Most widows have been thrust into female-headship at a very young age, and yet because of cultural factors they continue in this status quo throughout their lives... Economic survival and ensuring the welfare of our children is only one aspect of our existence. When you are thrust into female-headship at a tender age, as was my case, our sexual urges and needs remain. Though I am 38 years old, my sexual needs have been repressed since I was 29 years old... If female-heads take up religious matters, read prayer books, and so forth then she may be able to repress her needs. And some female-heads do take to religion fervently upon the death of their spouse... For the average female-head, therefore, the emphasis is on being mothers and widows and not women in their own right. And our culture continues to emphasize this again and again... My decision to continue my daughter's education, therefore, is done in the hope that she too will critically look at these issues. By being active in the community my hope is that I help create a space for her and other young women where cultural norms become lax, there are less restrictions placed on women, and women's needs and rights are recognized in holistic ways.
>
> (*Rajini, a 38-year old Tamil de jure female-head from Ampara, and mother of one daughter*).[35]

---

[35] This female-head was one of the few who touched upon issues that I had originally no intention of pursuing. Discussing issues of female sexuality during my fieldwork, I realized, was taboo. This was not because I subscribe to the view that sexual unions outside of marriage do not take place in rural communities, but

The decision to examine how the different dimensions of social and cultural practices link to issues of female-headship has been useful to my study. It helps accentuate the level of feminist consciousness some female heads did possessed. Their decisions on educating their children, especially daughters, therefore were an implicit challenge to patriarchal relations and maternalist ideology.

To conceive the social world as human-agency dependent, captures reality as differentiated and interconnected.[36] And the narration of female-heads and their decisions on children's welfare, I believe, elucidates this particular issue. Hence, this particular methodological point is well worth bearing in mind for feminist activism, which must seek to move beyond simple stories of social reality.

APPENDIX

A primary purpose of this paper is to draw upon the social, cultural, and ethnic norms of Muslim, Sinhalese and Tamil female-heads, so as to assess how economic decisions are shaped and influenced by these structural features in eastern Sri Lanka. This, however, is a task fraught with difficulty, because these differences do not have fixed and stable ethnic roots. By using ethnic markers the similarities as well as the differences across class and gender that inform economic decision-making are uncovered to illustrate the many instances in which female-heads — having socialized gender, class, social and ethno-nationalist identities — shape economic decision-making accordingly. While statistics unravel the particular economic positions of female-heads in each ethnic group, the socio-cultural context within which they work

---

rather that open discussion of such issues rarely occur. Yet, where female heads did broach this issue they convincingly tied it to their desire to make their daughters lives "better" than their own experiences.

[36] See Tony Lawson, *Economics and Reality* (London and New York: Routledge, 1997); "Feminism, Realism and Universalism," in *Feminist Economics* 5, no. 2 (1999): 25-59; "Ontology and Feminist Theorising," in *Feminist Economics* 9, no. 1 (2003):119-150.

out survival strategies and make economic choices is also important.

In order to appreciate these relationships there is a need to move away from orthodox survey questionnaire methods to more varied approaches to conducting research[37]. Questionnaires can be useful, but their limitations are many. Anthropologists initially raised similar concerns when feminists pointed to the androcentric assumptions that are at the core of the empirical survey tradition[38]. Feminist economists, too, have increasingly documented their reservations about relying on the questionnaire method, and have called for a broadening of the methods used in conducting research in economics[39].

Motivated by feminist economic scholarship, from my survey sample of 298 female-heads, 100 female-heads — approximately 30 to 35 female-heads from each ethnic group — were selected for in-depth dialogue. The research was conducted in Ampara, Batticaloa, and Trincomalee districts of eastern Sri Lanka, where I along with local women from each community and village carried out the quantitative survey. For the qualitative study, I made trips to specific villages that were noted as Muslim, Sinhala or Tamil in 'cleared', (i.e. state controled) areas of each district, which helped ensure the ethnic variation of the profiled female-heads. There was, however, no particular procedure for selecting the female-heads that were interviewed in depth, and usually many of the profiled female-heads were made through their contacts with various local non-governmental organizations or local political and women activists. In addition, conversations I had with women and others in the communities shaped and sharpened my perceptions of the issues of female-heads in the re-

---

[37] Martha MacDonald, "The Empirical Challenges of Feminist Economics: The example of economic restructuring," in *Out of the Margin: Feminist Perspectives on Economics*, eds., Edith Kuiper et al. (London: Routledge, 1995), 175-97.
[38] Edward R Leach, "An Anthropologist's Reflections on a Social Survey," in *Anthropologists in the Field*, eds., D. G. Jongmans and P.C.W. Gutkind, (Netherlands: Van Gorcum & Co, 1967), 75-88; Sandra Harding, The Science Question in Feminism (Milton Keynes: Open University Press, 1986), 24-6, 162.
[39] See MacDonald. See also *Feminist Economics* 3 no. 2, (1997): 121-25, 137-9, 141-51, 119-120, 131-35.

gion. Based on these case studies, in this paper, therefore, I discuss the complexities of social structures by paying explicit attention to the resources — i.e. children — that female-heads draw upon in their quest for making the lives of their families better.

As a feminist economist, my reservations about empirical techniques are many. This stance is not simply an outcome of my ideological commitment to broadening the feminist economics base, but also because my field experience made me more aware of the simplification and limitations of empirical methods.[40] Gender relationships have to be situated historically, socially, politically and culturally, and ethnographic studies as well as non-formal information gathering exercises are needed to capture the richness and complexity of such dynamics. Drawing upon conversations with female-heads and other women in these communities, I was able to get their impressions, thoughts and perceptions of their particular experiences. These narratives draw attention to the numerous ways in which female-heads maneuver structural context as well as their approach towards decision-making. Both these processes underscore the importance of social relationships and social/cultural mores in 'economic' decision-making.

Drawing upon narratives and qualitative research, therefore, helped tease out the diversity of female-heads' experiences that is important in understanding both the political economic contexts as well as cultural underpinnings of female-heads' decision-making processes. Indeed, economic development requires paying attention to structures that should be re-shaped through gender sensitive policy-making, and information about these can only be acquired through qualitative research.

Kanchana N. Ruwanpura *is a Humboldt Research Fellow at the Ludwig Maximilians University (Munich) in the the Department of Economics & the Post-Colonial Studies program. She completed her Ph.D at Newnham College, Cambridge in 2001.*

---

[40] Ruwanpura 2001:32-38

The Unconscious of Democracy: Ideological hegemony and nationalism in post-socialist Croatia

Ozren Pupovac

Abstract

This paper analyses the struggles on the terrain of ideology in Croatia in the context of the struggles over the legacy of the Yugoslav socialist federation. It attempts to demonstrate that this ideological terrain was complex and heterogeneous, and that it cannot be explained one-dimensionally, in terms of the dominance of a particular idea of 'ethno-nationalism'. Contrary to simplistic depictions of the rise of nationalist ideology, which, in their vulgar variants, use metaphors of mass manipulation, we would like to point to its role in the constitution of an ideological hegemony. We argue that the key to understanding the power of nationalist discourses should be sought in their ability to play a transversal function — to articulate a plurality of different political demands and popular discontents. In this sense, we point to the process of overdetermination of the signifier of 'democracy' in the course of the struggles over Croatian independence, which in our view functioned as an 'empty signifier' in the Laclauian sense — a signifier providing universal political representation. However, we also try to demonstrate how this political sequence involved a perversion of the democratic ideology, how a mode of universalist representation and its according institutions and mechanisms reproduced a new socio-political boundary in the Croatian society and legitimated the violence exerted towards the Serbian population. Finally, we try to show how these ambivalent ideological effects reverberate across the wider discussion concerning the historical field of nationalism.

The remarkable thing with categories like 'nationalism' in social sciences and philosophy is not merely their conceptual messiness, the way in which they arouse contradictions in the theoretical field in which they are defined. It is also the manner in which they can condense a series of spontaneous ideologies, the fact that their application can invoke a number of latent stereotypes or common-sense moralisms. Up to a certain point, this also means that these very scientific categories, surrounded as they usually are by some positivistic naivete, construct social hierarchies and express relations of power.

Indeed, 'nationalism' is one of the most obvious designations of the 'transitional' situation in Eastern Europe. Its scope is scalar, ranging from the optimism of the 'rebirth of democracy' to the pessimism of the 'ethnic conflicts' and wars in Yugoslavia. And yet the contradiction between the two poles of this scale seems to subvert the very consistency of the category of 'nationalism', which then backlashes on its own content. For haven't we seen already that the inability to account for this fatal leap lets loose too easily a certain 'ethnocentrism'? It is an 'ethnocentrism' that calls upon the division of the history of Europe, as well as the division of its social space, in two parts — the 'West' and the 'East'. This is a specific division, for not only are the parts represented as absolutely heterogeneous to each other, but there is also a clear hierarchy between them. The 'East', according to this scheme, is a category that subsumes the peoples and social spaces which cannot be detached from their own particularity, from their specific 'culture' and 'ethnos'; in contrast to the 'West', which is represented as the bearer of the universal. Through this matrix, 'nationalism' is read as an almost exclusive property of the 'East', of the spaces and populations where politics cannot be uttered universally.

This duality is what we find behind the attachment of the prefix 'ethno-' to the analyses of 'nationalism' in the 'East'. The prefix functions here as an ideological corrective, offering an interpretation for the paradoxes and betrayals of the 'transition' — for the historical (re)emergence of nationalism on the European periphery and its deviations and perversities. And it does so not only by detecting the pervasiveness of certain political ideas in the current situation, such as that of the 'ethnic nation' or *Kulturnation,* but also by giving 'ethnographic' reasons for the permanence of these 'anachronisms'. This explanation involves a double distortion. On the one hand, it blends together history and anthropology, explaining a historical and political particularism through a particularist historiography. On the other hand, it reduces the very complexity of the situation. It obscures the fact that it was the very universalistic jargon of 'democracy', 'liberty' and 'self-determination' that carried the waves of political transformations in the 'East' at the beginning of the nineties.

In the following text, we propose to take a different look at the situation. We would like to account for this contradiction between the 'universalist' and the 'particularist' *topoi* of nationalism by analysing the struggles on the terrain of ideology which are taking place in the political context of Croatia at the dusk of the Yugoslav socialist federation in the early nineties. And in this regard, we will be fairly reductive, for we will only touch upon the dominant political discourses and those commonplaces that signified the general trajectories of political affairs in this context. Nevertheless, we will attempt to demonstrate the political and historical significance of this rhetoric. From the point of view of the theory of ideology, the questions that we would like to pose in relation to this situation are that of the effectivity of discourses and doctrines, their role in the generation of a social tie, of producing the cohesive effect. Our thesis is that the rise and the dominance of nationalism at the beginning of the nineties in Croatia cannot be reduced to a single principle, a single idea, but that this political situation was far more complex, that it consisted of political and intellectual interventions oriented around the formation of an ideological hegemony. In this sense, we argue that the tension between 'universality' and 'particularity' is, in fact, an expression of the struggle around the constitution of a socio-political unity around a set of different political positions and contradictory social processes, a struggle over the articulation of a number of different principles of legitimation, political demands and popular discontents. In addition to their 'constructive' role, we would like to demonstrate the destructive side of these ideological tensions, how they were inscribed in the entire struggle over the Yugoslav legacy, how they helped create new social divisions in Croatian society and to exacerbate conflicts, specifically the conflict between the new Croatian regime and the Serbian population living under its jurisdiction.

*   *   *

Let us start by looking at a peculiar slogan which emerged amongst many excited and enthusiastic voices announcing the 're-birth of democracy' in Croatia. Shortly before Croatia's first post-communist parliamentary elections in the spring of 1990, the political party led by Tudman, the HDZ, decided to promote itself through a laconic statement: 'Our name is our programme!'

Interestingly, one is first provoked to note that the political context in which parties stress their names instead of political interests or articulated programmes seems an aberration of the norm of representative democracy — presuming that the autonomous political sphere ought to represent different positions of social groups and their interests. Does this mean that we are dealing here, with an 'irrational' moment of history, that is, the history of democratic forms and practices, or simply an example of an obscure accident, an unexplainable historical contingency? Can we speak of an absence of the proper subject of 'political representation' in this slogan? Or is there a specific political rationality underlying it?

In order to approach this peculiarity, let us presume that the HDZ was politically sober when making its proclamation, and thus try to reconstruct the meaning that the potential addressees of the statement are to grasp from the very name of this political party — the meaning that could eventually influence their voting decisions. The acronym HDZ stands for '*Hrvatska demokratska zajednica*', which reads in English as 'the Croatian Democratic Community'.[1] It is easy to decipher the political meaning of two of the elements of this abbreviation. Clearly, both the adjective 'Croatian' and the noun 'community' stand out as commonplaces of nationalist discourses. The adjective 'Croatian' pronounces and emphasizes the name of the 'nation' and thus already presumes a specific addressee of this party, and, conse-

---

[1] The most commonly accepted translation of the acronym HDZ is 'Croatian Democratic Union' or CDU. For the purposes of this analysis, however, we have decided to preserve the literal meaning of the Croatian noun 'zajednica', which primarily denotes a 'community', but could also mean an 'association' or 'union'.

quently, sets a limit on those whom it seeks to represent.[2] These are the individuals belonging to the 'Croatian nation', or, more exactly, the 'Croats'.[3] The noun 'community', presumably, denotes the character of this addressee. That is, it addresses the Croats as a 'community', a political conception which often involves several idealizations expressed through metaphors borrowed from biology. This would mean here that the 'community of Croats' rests on the image of an organic unity (a corporeal metaphor) and a fantasy about the continuity of genus (a community of kin). But the adjective 'democratic' stands out somehow in this syntagm; it seems, so to say, out of place. It is not an ordinary mannerism of the romantic nationalist repertoire which is evoked here, and, moreover, one is tempted to observe that today, after the tragic historical experience of his rule, it sounds paradoxical at least to claim that Tuđman and his political party embodied the virtues and principles of democracy. So what determines the place and the role of 'democracy' in the very name of the political party that won political power in Croatia in the early nineties?

In order to further explore this ambiguity let us take a look at another utterance spoken by the same authority, in which the locus of 'democracy' seems even more mysterious:

> 'They [the Croatian Serbs] are attempting to bring about a scenario aimed at demolishing the democracy that we have established'[4]

It is not so easy to make sense of this statement. What is exactly meant by the term 'democracy' which is under threat of

---

[2] It is important to note here, however, that the over-emphasis on the particular national identity was not only characteristic for Tuđman's party. In fact, most of the political parties formed at the beginning of the nineties in Croatia, whether of 'left' or 'right' orientation, included the adjective 'Croatian' in their names (e.g. Croatian Party of Right, Croatian Peasants' Party, Social Democratic Party of Croatia, Croatian People's Party, etc.). A similar process could be traced in almost all post-Yugoslav political contexts.

[3] There is an idiosyncrasy of the context which should be stressed here, because the term 'narod' in the Serbo-Croatian language does not make a difference between the 'people' and the 'nation'.

[4] Franjo Tuđman cited in *Vjesnik*, 30 October 1990.

demolition by the Serbs in Croatia? It would be hard to presume that the 'democracy' whose existence is in danger here involves the ideal of the 'egalitarian rule of the people', because of the fact that the Serbs, still living in large numbers on the territory of the Croatian Republic at the time of the enunciation of this statement, would constitute a part of the formal political category of the 'people' and would have to have a share in the rule of the 'popular will'. Additionally, it is difficult to read this element of the utterance with the help of certain synonyms or syntagmas that are promulgated in today's hegemonic political discourses, that is, as 'liberal-democracy'. The Croatian Serbs, who comprised twelve percent of the population of Croatia at the beginning of the nineties, could have hardly represented a threat to the idea of the *Rechtsstaat* (the Rule of Law, or what would simply be the liberal State), to the ideology of individual rights and liberties, to the juridico-political figure of the abstract individual, for they would have to be considered as individual members of a polity or a state built upon such foundations, and moreover, members which as 'men and citizens' possess specific rights and freedoms to safeguard and express their 'identity' through the mechanisms of representative democracy.

Let us expose the political situation here. The utterance is, in fact, spoken in the course of the escalation of the conflict between the newly elected leadership of the Croatian state and the militant representatives of Croatian Serbs, which concerned the questions of the definition of the new political order and its relation to the Yugoslav federation. But also, this political context is decisively marked by a thorough transformation of the political institutions in Croatia, following the wider process of the 'democratic transition' taking place not only in Yugoslavia but throughout the socialist regimes in the East of Europe, which means that the signifier 'democracy' could in fact refer to the introduction of a set of democratic institutions and mechanisms — the parliamentary political system, multi-party elections, the rule of law and the separation of powers, freedom of media and expression, freedom of association, etc. But then again, we would have to note the ambiguity that is created between the 'ideals' inscribed in these institutions and their concrete materialization in the Croatian context, where a significant part of the population living on the territory that is ruled by the aforementioned democratic means, the Croatian Serbs, do not equally share access to those means, but are seen as a fundamental threat to them.

Of course, one could observe that the problem here simply hinges upon a definition of the external and internal boundaries of democratic rule, and the questions of the division of the polity, or 'majorities' and 'minorities'. But this is exactly what is left un-problematised and thus obscured in this statement, or rather, this is what should be presumed both by the speaker and the address-ees as self-evident in order for the utterance to have a meaning. And in fact, this is where the catch lies — in the specific way in which an ideological discourse resonates in this utterance. The ideological effect or the sense of this statement is generated by evoking the silent assumption that the speaker and the ideal ad-dressee share an assumption about the boundaries of democratic rule. Such boundaries do not come naturally nor are they inevita-ble. Rather, they are most commonly the product of a political decision or a historical force. But they do have to be naturalised, presented as self-evident and necessary truths in order to be effec-tive; this 'mystification' of origins is one of the primary operations of the ideological discourse.[5]

Let us put things bluntly now: 'democracy' implied in the statement of the Croatian President is ambiguous because it is tainted with a particular content — it does in fact refer to a set of political institutions and political ideals, but their universalist, so to say, empty content, is limited to a particular, in this case 'cul-turally' defined group; the Croats. In order to interpret this utter-ance the ideal addressee has to assume that the boundaries of the *demos*, of the political community in which she or he lives, coin-cide with the boundaries of his or her *ethnos*, that is, the commu-nity in which he or she belongs through an imagined ancestry. In such a way, we have detected one operation of the hegemonic ide-

---

[5] As Michel Pêcheux has shown in his remarkable elaboration of the Althusserian theory of ideology, one of the central characteristics of ideological discourse is the production of the 'self-evidence' of meaning. See Michel Pêcheux, *Language, Semantics and Ideology* (London: Macmillan Press, 1982).

ology in Croatia at the beginning of the nineties — it imposes a particular adjective over a formal empty substantive, or, in political terms, a particularistic and essentialist definition of peoplehood over the one which is defined by formal political institutions, such as citizenship and universal suffrage. 'Democracy' reads here as 'Croatian democracy', as the rule of the majority nation, the rule of the 'general will' where the Croatian Serbs, as members of a different 'culturally' defined entity, that is, as Serbs, do not have their equal share.

If we return to the assertion of *nomen est omen* by the HDZ, we can now show how the ambiguous adjective 'democratic' figures in their peculiar political slogan. The signifier 'democracy' is dislocated here: it is, so to say, divorced from its 'habitual meaning' and its sense is generated by the articulation with the other two elements of the acronym HDZ. If we put it in the spirit of the theoretical language implied here we can say that 'democracy' is *overdetermined* — its meaning is a product of processes of condensation and displacement. This means that one can properly read 'democracy' in HDZ's name only in relation to, and that is, in excessive relation to the adjective 'Croatian' and the noun 'community'. The signifier 'democracy' underlines the political significance of 'culture', that is, it pronounces the political demand of 'national self-determination' — which is a demand, as Gellner accurately observed, based upon the idea of the congruence of political and cultural borders.[6] In other words, 'democracy' here functions as a metaphor for the idea of 'national sovereignty'. Therefore, we can contend that there is a specific political rationality behind this awkward slogan, that the political agenda or the programme that is 'hidden' in the very name of Tuđman's political party is that of the popular sovereignty of the nationally constituted community. In the Yugoslav federal context in the early nineties, that is, in the context of the crisis of its political and ideological underpinnings, this was a demand for the redefinition of its elementary political communities, the (socialist)

---

[6] See Ernest Gellner, *Nations and Nationalism* (Oxford: Blackwell, 1983).

republics, as well as the demand for the redefinition (or the negation) of the federal terrain as such.

*   *   *

We should expand the analytical process here, because the
precedent interpretation seems obviously insufficient. Even
though we have managed to discern the logic behind the ambiguity of the term at the level of signification, the question still remains : why do the Croatian nationalists — Tuđman and the
HDZ — in both of these cases need 'democracy'? Why is an ambiguous and seemingly superfluous element present in these historical utterances? What were the practical and political effects of
these rhetorical uses? A compelling way to approach these problems was proposed by Ernesto Laclau, who in conceptualizing the
weight of rhetorical elements in politics stressed that we need to
distinguish between the literal content and the proper political
meaning of signs. In elaborating on this difference, he introduced
the concept of the *empty signifier*, a signifier without a signified,
whose only function is to represent the unity of the entire field of
signification. As Laclau writes: "there can be empty signifiers
within the field of signification because any system of signification is structured around an empty place resulting from the impossibility of producing an object which, none the less, is required
by the systematicity of the system".[7]

---

[7] Ernesto Laclau, *Emancipation(s)* (London: Verso, 1996), 40. The logical attributes of the concept of the 'empty signifier' can be exposed by a difference that
Laclau attempts to establish between his concept and that of the 'floating signifier'. As we know, the concept of the 'floating signifier' theorizes the impossibility
of a 'totality' — it points to the inherent ambiguity of the sign produced by an
excess or a deficiency of the signifieds (in Lacanian language: 'the sliding of the
signified under the signifier' which is being constantly generated by the infinity of
the process of signification). By extension more than by contrast, the concern
around the concept of the empty signifier is exactly that of the necessity of 'totality'. The question of the totality of the signifying system and thus of its limits is
logically necessary because, as Saussure teaches us, every act of signification involves the totality of language, or rather, the constitution of each particular differential relation within the system necessitates the existence of an object which
could represent this totality. However, as Laclau reasons, such an object cannot
be represented directly, because in such a case it would be already included in the

As we know, in transposing this formal reasoning to the terrain of history and politics, Laclau is indebted to Gramscian analyses of *hegemony* and the specific scene of political struggles which this notion implies. The concept of hegemony elaborated in Gramsci's *Quaderni del carcere* points to a power relation which is not based upon coercion, such as the control over the means of violence, but is founded upon the production of consent, of bringing together, or to put it in terms of the theoretical language evoked here, of *articulating* different political interests, beliefs, values and demands of the actors involved around a common site.[8] Thus, *hegemony* is not in any way reducible to state power and its 'repressive apparatuses' (the police, law, the military, etc.), but involves a much broader and pluralistic scene — that of the multiplicity of struggles and vehicles of these struggles present in 'civil society'. By locating *hegemony* in social practices such as intellectual interventions in 'public opinion', forms of mass media and popular culture, educational institutions, numerous cultural associations, religious organizations, as well as social movements and trade unions, Gramsci radically expands the scope of our understanding of power relations and thus of the making of history. For Gramsci, the field of 'cultural politics' is crucial; he depicts a scene of politics where the decisive acts are the acts of intellectual, moral and philosophical leadership; in this sense, the struggle over *hegemony* is directed at winning the 'hearts and the minds of the people', it consists of those interventions into the 'social consciousness' that attempt to construct a universal platform, a 'general will', to create the 'fundamental outlook for the whole society'.

In accordance with this conception of politics, 'empty signifiers' are the primary vehicles of power relations, that is, hegemonic relations. They are the ideological objects which unify the

---

differential play of signification. Empty signifiers emerge precisely at this point, whereby one particular element of the signifying system subverts its own differential location within the system and starts representing the (absence of the) totality as such. See 'Why do Empty Signifiers Matter to Politics?' in Laclau, 36-47.
[8] See Antonio Gramsci, *Selections from the Prison Notebooks* (New York: International Publishers, 1999), especially the chapters 'The Modern Prince', 123-205, and 'State and Civil Society', 206-276. [modified citation]

forces and the stakes of the political struggle, the objects which perform the function of universal representation within a political context or a political situation. The 'emptying of a signifier' is a political and ideological process by which an element of political rhetoric — a slogan, a demand, a value, a representation or a moral judgement loses the weight of its particularity and becomes the vacant metaphorical surface that can create a community over the contradictions between the positions, actors, agendas and interests involved in the political struggles out of which it emerges. A signifier is not empty because it doesn't have a meaning at all, or because anyone can at her own free will and according to different definitions of the communicational situation attribute a meaning to it; it is empty because within a concrete political context its literal meaning — a particular proclamation or a demand attached to a group pronouncing it — is being metaphorically transposed in order to perform a 'transversal function' — to represent the consent of the parties involved and the unity of their particular interests. Additionally, 'empty signifiers' do not merely concern political alliances, but perform one of the crucial roles of the reproduction of social relations writ large by generating what Althusser called 'the society effect'.[9] Consequently, the proper political meaning of rhetorical figures emerges from the gap between their particular content and their empty 'universalist' role (the ordering of the heterogeneous social field) — and this gap is the space where struggles over hegemony are being fought.[10]

*   *   *

---

[9] For a brilliant theoretical elaboration of the role of the extra-economic coercion in the reproduction of capitalist relations see Louis Althusser and Étienne Balibar *Reading Capital* (London: New Left Books, 1970).

[10] Laclau gives an illustrative example of this operation: "Let us suppose that workers' mobilization succeeds in presenting its own objectives as a signifier of 'liberation' in general. In one sense this is a hegemonic victory, because the objectives of a particular group are identified with society at large. But, in another sense, this is a dangerous victory. If 'workers' struggle' becomes the signifier of liberation as such, it also becomes the surface of inscription through which all liberating struggles will be expressed, so that the chain of equivalences which are unified around this signifier tend to empty it, and to blur its connection with the actual content with which it was originally associated", (Laclau, 45).

Can we contend that 'democracy' functioned as an empty signifier in Croatia at the end of the eighties and the beginning of the nineties? If we explore the minutiae of this historical and ideological context, such an interpretation seems indeed plausible. Caught up in the same wave of restructurings of the capitalist world-system as its 'Eastern' socialist neighbours,[11] the Yugoslav socialist federation, and Croatia as part of it, crumbled under the pressures that sought to introduce capitalist modes of production and political rule into the society. In the decade of the eighties, and especially its latter part, this social context was ridden with numerous transformations at the levels of politics and ideology, closely intertwined with those taking place at the 'economic base' of the society. The general moments of the ideological edifice that supported the federal construction created by the Yugoslav Communist Party after the Second World War — such as the political slogan of 'brotherhood and unity' that emerged during the course of the anti-fascist struggle, and later the humanist and federalists principles of 'self-management socialism' and the internationalist project of the 'non-alignment' — came to be perceived as reference points without any substance whatsoever. Also, the legal-political and institutional framework that was oriented towards the redistribution and reciprocity between the (national) societies which composed Yugoslavia, as well as making possible the 'balance of powers' within the federal state, began to disintegrate under the increasing disagreements amongst the republican elites of the Party which put forth particularistic demands. In this context of crisis, the language of 'reforms' hyped up the political *nomenklatura* in different Yugoslav republics — instead of the commonplaces of the socialist rhetoric which now seemed out of place, the political class of Yugoslavia started increasingly expressing itself through the alluring jargon of the 'transition' and its buzzwords like 'pluralism', 'market economy', 'Europeanisation' and 'democ-

---

[11] See Immanuel Wallerstein, *The Modern World-System* (3 vols.) (Cambridge: Cambridge University Press, 1974-89); and also his Geopolitics and Geoculture: Essays on the changing world-system (Cambridge: Cambridge University Press, 1991).

ratisation'. But apart from this sudden and serene gesture which transformed the rulers from socialist 'cadres' into the liberal 'technocrats', the political stage in Yugoslavia witnessed the heterogenisation and pluralisation of voices, whereby the symptoms of the 'democratic bubble' could be discerned in the multiple requests for 'democratic pluralism', 'freedom of speech' and 'human and civil rights' which were announcing the pressures from 'below'. Parallel to the political milieu of the Eastern European 'velvet revolutions' where the signifier 'democracy' represented one of the fundamental grounds for the mobilization and the organization of the social movements and other actors engaged in the struggle against the apparatuses of power of the regimes that were named 'really existing socialisms', the political scene of Yugoslavia in the eighties witnessed the birth of a plethora of different anti-establishment struggles emerging from the arena of the popular — from student protests, feminist struggles, identitary movements, peace and human rights campaigns, workers' struggles through trade unions and strikes, cultural and religious concerns, public opinion involvements, intellectual and academic interventions, to the new political groupings which tended to displace the dominance of the communist led one-party system.

It is this historical and political context that Rastko Močnik rightly labelled as "democratic evangelisation",[12] a context in which the idiom of 'democracy' and its ideological programmatic twins — 'civil society' and 'political pluralism' — seemed to have preoccupied the entire endeavour of politics, providing a cheerful and march-like gospel of historical importance and collective salvation. However, such an omnipresent reference point was not rid of absurdities. The signifier 'democracy' was almost simultaneously the locus of several different political struggles and the ground for a number of contradictory political processes. Firstly, it preoccupied the most prominent place in the struggles in the sphere of 'civil society', in the popular resistance against socialist regimes and in the movements and aspirations of 'direct democracy' aimed against the dictates and the pedagogy of the state.

---

[12] Rastko Močnik, *Fragments on Identitary Argumentation in Post-Political Discourse* (unpublished manuscript, 2003)

However, one could also find an inversion of this function of 'democracy' as anti-establishment resistance and critique — 'democracy' simultaneously became the ideological medium through which the Yugoslav post-socialist states themselves, or more exactly, their 'reformist' regimes, were preparing the terrain for a dramatic social transformation, stacking legitimacy for their role as the arbiters of the capitalist relations of production and as the executors of the new forms of authority bound to secure the former. The third occupation of the idiom of democracy occurs, nonetheless, in the moment when the state apparatus and its formal juridico-political language proves unable to cultivate the contradictions brought about by the new forms of dependencies and domination and when help was sought in various modalities of excess, both physical and symbolic, with their foundations equally in the civil society struggles and the state institutions themselves. On this excessive ideologico-political surface, 'democracy' starts being presented though the filter of the nationalist ideology.

It is not difficult to trace the line along which hegemonic relations are being constituted in such a situation. The signifier 'democracy' figures as a medium of integration, as an empty signifier in the Laclauian sense, in the interplay of these different social positions and political projects. It unifies the heterogeneous and even contradictory set of actors, interests and demands and it manages to generate consent between different centres of power, institutional spheres and their according discourses. In political parlance, it becomes an empty rhetorical phrase that could be inserted into any political discourse with instantaneous results.

It is exactly in this sense that we should read the rhetoric of the ruling party in Croatia at the beginning of the nineties. The element of 'democracy' that we find in the statements of the Croatian nationalists is but a moment in the formation of an ideological hegemony, and thus a factor of social and political cohesion. Towards the 'inside' of the political context in Croatia, the rhetoric of 'democracy' the new nationalist regime to produce consent by drawing a 'chain of equivalences' — to use Laclau's vocabulary — between different socio-political positions, thus restructuring the relationships between the political class, the state apparatuses and the masses. The universal reach of 'democracy' provided the link for new 'adversaries' in the arena of parliamentary politics — the reformed communists qua social democrats, the liberals and the nationalists — but also, it offered a common platform for the actors and interests both on the formal political scene of liberal-democratic institutions and the 'unmediated' expressions of democracy stemming from 'civil alternatives'.[13] By unifying the entire spectrum of the political sphere, the new regime established and secured its power, its ability to define the general course of political affairs, and to push forward its programmes and policies without much resistance. In short, it managed to generate widespread consensus and mass consent. This hegemonic effectiveness of 'democracy', its adhesive potential, can be straightforwardly read from the fact that the pre-war government of the post-communist Croatia, a government which united the differences between the ruling party and the opposition, and which unequivocaly supported to the political programmes of national sovereignty and state independence, was called the 'government of democratic unity'.

As an element of ideological hegemony, 'democracy' proved to be a powerful legitimating device, not only towards the 'inside', but also towards the 'outside', on the terrain of international politics and in the eyes of the numerous observers from the 'West'. In the midst of the euphoria around the collapse of Eastern European 'real socialisms' it was easy to seek political support through the jargon of 'democratic revolutions', to refer to the events such as the 'fall of the Berlin Wall' and the 'velvet revolutions' in Poland and Czechoslovakia. As we know, these events touched upon the cornerstone of values of the Western capitalist states — the universality of the modern democratic gesture. What

---

[13] A couple of months after the 1990 elections, non-party intellectuals affiliated to one of the major 'oppositional' parties at the beginning of the nineties, the Coalition of National Agreement (KNS), issued a written declaration in support of the general course of politics defined by the new regime: 'We believe that political and ideological differences, characteristic of each democratic and pluralist society, would not be an obstacle to the fact that all political parties, that all Croatian citizens would unite in the struggle for the defence of the democratic and sovereign Croatia, as well as the defence of the will of the Croatian nation, expressed on the last multi-party elections'; cited from: Joža Vlahović, *"Danas" 1982 — 1992*, (Rijeka: Novi List, 2002), 132.

was widely celebrated as the 'rebirth of history', appealed to its observers as the repetition of the historical act that was constitutive of European political modernity — the assertion of 'We the people', of 'popular sovereignty' against the *ancien régime* — brought about by the French and the American bourgeois revolutions. In the post-socialist context, the motif of the 'struggle against tyranny' that the Jacobins called for was repeated in the 'struggle against communism'. It posited the 'sovereignty of the people', a political insurrection, against the 'real socialist' regimes and the one-party system, and later, in a somewhat ironic way, served as a legitimating device for the establishment of new regimes and new states on the basis of anti-communist ideology.

By representing its actions and policies as 'democratic', by appealing to the universality of 'democratic revolutions' and the 'overthrow of communism' the political class in Croatia legitimated its programmes and policies, and in this sense, it managed to gain support for and even to naturalise the call for political independence. In the eyes of the 'West', of most of the parties in the global context of *Realpolitik* that were related to this situation, the state construct that was being built out of the Yugoslav federation appeared as the triumph and the expression of the 'democratic will', as opposed to the phantasmatic referent of 'communist one-party dictatorship'. But as we indicated before, there was a deformation of the imagery that related to the foundational gestures of the modern political subjectivity. Croatian nationalists did not attribute sovereignty to the 'people' but to the 'nation', a political community which was united 'organically', by an imagined kinship. The nationalist optics of the new Croatian regime distorted the image of the 'democratic revolutions' by attaching a particular content to the 'popular sovereign', by transforming the political consensus into a 'national consensus' and thus by defining the internal and external limits of 'democracy' in terms of the 'majority nation'. The meaning of the term 'democratisation' in the Croatian political context in the early nineties was more or less coextensive with the claim for the sovereignty of the Croatian nation.

There was a force of historical tragedy, or even farce, in these proceedings. For the idiom of 'democracy' was not only constructive, i.e., it did not merely function in terms of social co-hesion and consensus building. It also served as an ideological gospel that legitimated the authoritarian measures and the excess of violence which followed the establishment of post-socialist states. In the closing phase of the 'democratic brew', the newly established democratic governments have managed to destroy those autonomous spaces which were fought for through the plu-rality and the polyphony of 'popular-democratic' struggles. Whilst proclaiming their authority and seeking their legitimacy in panic, the political regimes emerging out of the crumbling of Yugoslav socialism, and now wearing theatrical nationalist dresses, have forcefully assaulted civil-society actors, by suffocating the possi-bilities of critical voice through the limitations of media expres-sion, by resurrecting the patriarchal conservative morality of 'church, family and duty', by elevating their rule above and out-side the legitimate confines of the *Rechtsstaat,* by persecuting the ethnic and national minorities living on the territories under their jurisdiction, by implementing 'racialist' cultural policies, by con-demning strike activities and workers' demands, to name only some examples.

In the following section, we will attempt to examine some elements of the conflictual scenery behind the idiom of 'democ-racy' in the Yugoslav post-socialist context. But first, we should introduce a 'comparative perspective'. The fact that these destruc-tive acts cannot be read as simple historical accidents on the (semi)periphery of the world-system is the symmetry exhibited in the form of the extra-economic coercion — a combination of the feasting by the repressive apparatuses and the all-round mobilisa-tion of the ideological apparatuses of the state — to that exerted throughout the eighties in the capitalist societies of the 'centre' under the banners of neo-liberal ideologies. The analyses of the Thatcherite strategy by the Marxist-oriented social sciences in Britain, and most notably the concept of 'authoritarian populism' suggested by Stuart Hall, beget the disturbing analogy with the post-Yugoslav context.[14] It would not be redundant to remind ourselves that within the changing economic, institutional and geopolitical landscape of the world-system in the late seventies and eighties, the reaction to the crisis by the neo-liberal right represented by the Thatcherite government in Britain was the increase of state interventions and the expansion of its 'policing function' resulting in the brutal repression of trade union activities and the assault on the instruments of welfare secured in the Keynesian state-model. As the analyses of Hall and others have shown, such 'authoritarian' interventions of the state were sanctioned and legitimised by a cynical gesture of denial — by the anti-étatist rhetoric aimed at the welfare system and the political representation of labour, which was additionally strengthened by elevating the classical ideological elements of liberalism such as the 'free-market', 'self-interest' and 'competitive individualism'. But the most important thing to note is that the strategy of Thatcherism 'took democracy seriously' — it sought to intervene in the field of 'democratic struggles', meaning that it directly resonated with a range of popular discontents, attitudes and commonplaces in aiming to constitute ideological hegemony. This was played out through vigorous ideological involvement around a number of general representations within the sphere of 'popular morality', such as the racist projections of British 'national identity' and the fabrication of 'moral panic' through a set of stigmatizations, packaged together, of course, with a set of conservative moral prescriptions.

---

[14] See Stuart Hall, *The Hard Road to Renewal: Thatcherism and the Crisis of the Left*, (London: Verso, 1988). Hall defines 'authoritarian populism' as 'an exceptional form of the capitalist state which, unlike classical fascism, has retained most (though not all) of the formal representative institutions in place, and which at the same time has been able to construct around itself an active popular consent' (Hall, 42). This contradictory strategy exhibits elements of 'authoritarian' rule — a conservative outlook, the emphasis on the strong state, the curtailment of formal liberties and the active use of the violent policing function, coupled with the tendency to control the every increasing spheres of socio-economic life — and of 'populist' politics — the fact that it 'takes democracy seriously', or seeks to attract the active consent of the popular masses through the ideological recuperation of common-sense perceptions and popular discontents.

*   *   *

The claims on behalf of 'national sovereignty' were not something exclusive to the leadership of Croatia, but were, in fact, more or less contemporaneously forwarded by the political elites of the majority of political entities of Yugoslavia (republics and provinces), in most cases unilaterally and arrogantly, at the expense and through the exclusion of others. Through the 'anticommunist' rhetoric, these projects aggravated the demolition of the terrain of the Yugoslav federation, together with its ideologies of solidarity and mutuality, and the mechanisms of redistribution and welfare built during the communist rule. But the programmes of 'national sovereignty' carried an explicitly contradictory element. Within the frames of the political, social, economic and cultural reality inherited from the Yugoslav federation — and mostly in relation to the fact that it consisted of multinational political entities or that the borders and the constituencies of its republics were 'culturally impure'[15] — there was an immense potential for a violent 'acting out' if such projects were sought to be implemented. And it was exactly this strategy which completely permeated the policies of the political leaderships of different Yugoslav republics, with some of them fortifying and closing the borders of their territorial jurisdiction, and others even seeking to purify and expand these by violent means — at first by the ideological machine through which those nationally 'impure elements' were stigmatised and discriminated, and later by the military machine which exacerbated the antagonisms turning them into local-imperialist wars followed by extreme forms of violence such as ethnic cleansing and mass murders.

---

[15] The political bodies constituted in the course of the communist-led anti-fascist struggle and later embodied in the documents and the institutions of the socialist federation were of a very peculiar form. The post-war, 1945 federal constitution of Yugoslavia created six republics, but with multiple bases of sovereignty. For example, the Socialist Republic of Croatia was defined as the state of the Croats and the Serbian population living on its territory, the sovereign body of the Socialist Republic of Bosnia and Herzegovina was composed of three national groups. In addition to 'republican sovereignty', the Yugoslav Federation as a whole was understood as the federal state of all of its constitutive 'nations' and 'nationalities', 'citizens' and also the 'entire working people of Yugoslavia'.

The new constitutional definitions that the nationalist regime in Croatia put forward did not attempt to hide the fact that the 'body politic', and the claims on statehood made on its behalf, differ from the totality of the population that comprises the territory of the republic. Quite the contrary, they made that explicit. In December 1990, the new Croatian constitution defined Croatia as the 'national state of the Croatian nation and the state of the members of autochthonous national minorities'. As we note here, the category of the 'sovereign people' is not constituted politically, by the institution of citizenship for example, but organically, with reference to an imagined community united by 'kinship' or 'culture'. The fundamental problem with this way of reconstituting the political order was that new lines of demarcation were introduced into the Croatian society, with the essential border being drawn along 'identitary' lines. The claim for a state construct on the basis of 'national sovereignty' had, at its limits, the Serbian population as the primary 'autochthonous nationality' living on the territory of the Croatian republic. The Croatian Serbs enjoyed a specific political status accredited by the Titoist federative order — that of the co-constitutional nation of the Socialist Republic of Croatia. The AVNOJ (*Antifascist Council of the People's Liberation of Yugoslavia*) documents that emerged during the course of the anti-fascist struggle, and the consecutive constitutions of the socialist Yugoslavia recognised the Croatian Serbs in the preambles of constitutional texts of the Croatian republic, as well as in the definitions of the sovereign political body.[16] By contrast, the new constitutional definitions stripped the Serbs in Croatia of the equal political status and constitutional rights and relegated them to the category of a 'national minority'.

The institution of this symbolic boundary paved the way for a conflict over the administrative-territorial apparatuses with the Serb population and its political representatives. In the locali-

---

[16] The 1974 constitution, for example, defined Croatia as the state of 'the Croatian nation, the state of the Serbian nation in Croatia and the state of the nationalities who live in it'. At the same time, however, it was the state 'based upon the sovereignty of the people and the rule and the self-management of the working class and all working people, as well as the socialist self-governing democratic community of working people, citizens, equal nations and nationalities'.

ties where the Serbs were the majority, the militant political leaderships openly boycotted the nationalist government and contested its authority. As a response to the programmes of state independence based on the sovereignty of the Croatian nation, claims for cultural and political autonomy were being put forward on behalf of the Croatian Serbs, also encircled by nationalist rhetoric. There were plans for secession from Croatia and unification with Serbia, if Croatia were to secede from Yugoslavia. And yet we should not forget here the overdetermination of this conflict, the fact that this 'internal' demarcation line was at the same time an 'external' one. The clash between the Croatian state and the Serbs was already inscribed in the wider conflict around the legacy of the Yugoslav federation. It reflected the struggles between different instances of authority of the crumbling federal order and especially the antagonism between the political leaderships of the republics over the questions of constitutional jurisdictions, popular sovereignty, citizenship and boundaries. The question of 'internal' sovereignty in Croatia was thus also the stake in the conflict between the new regimes in Croatia and Slovenia and and the leadership of Serbia. The former which proclaimed the independence of their republics on the basis of 'national sovereignty' and demanded the confederate reorganisation of relations in Yugoslavia. The latter who denied these claims, while seeking to redraw the boundaries of the federal institutions and republics under a nationalist agenda and forwarding its plan for a centralised Yugoslav state. Correspondent to the strategy of political homogenisation by way of 'culture' in Croatia and Slovenia, an analogous totalising ideology was more or less contemporaneously being generated by Serbia's political and intellectual leadership, also fuelling nationalist mythologies and xenophobic projections. The other Yugoslav republics, as well as the 'autonomous provinces' were not slow to follow these strategies. In such a situation, the paradoxical Serbian element in Croatia came to represent a direct collision between radically opposed, but nevertheless strikingly symmetrical political and ideological programmes. This created an 'impossible' relationship in which both sides were interlocked in the exchange of xenophobic stereotypes, endorsed the logic of blaming and demonisation, and resorted to discrimination and violence. The tragedy of the historical aftermath of these antagonistic political and ideological strategies is only too well known — the conflict erupted into an armed rebellion, later turning into an all-out 'civil-war' infecting the entirety of the post-Yugoslav social space and serving as a playground for a number of 'petty-imperialist' military projects.

There are many horrifying enigmas lying behind these developments, the most outstanding ones being the acute forms of subjective violence — mutilations, torture, raping and mass murders — surrounding the military conquests and armed resistance in the conflicts in Croatia and Bosnia and Herzegovina, as well as the struggles in Kosovo and Macedonia. Yet another striking fact is the swiftness through which nationalist antagonisms were built up, the incredible momentum with which feelings of hatred, fear, suspicion, violence and exclusion started founding social relations between different Yugoslav nations, thus replacing the experience of solidarity and mutuality built up during a half century of life in a common state. In this respect, the flaring up of the conflict in Croatia attracts particular attention.

Apart from the symbolic gesture which inscribed a 'cultural' boundary into the juridico-political documents of the Croatian state and paved the way for a political conflict, a whole set of emergent discourses and practices could be traced in Croatia at the beginning of the nineties, explicitly or implicitly sanctioned by the state, which were fortifying political antagonisms and transforming it into what Fichte once called the 'internal boundary'.[17] We would like to point here to the process of production of a complex of dispositions, attitudes, prejudices and behaviours which gravitates upon the most fundamental place in the cognitive and psychic life of individuals — their constitution as subjects. In this sense, Louis Althusser presented us with a remarkable formula for the processes of production of *individuality* and *subjectivity* in relation to practices of everyday life and the

---

[17] See Balibar's discussion of Fichte's Addresses to the German Nation and their significance for contemporary problematisations of the relation between capitalism and nationalism in Étienne Balibar, *Masses, Classes, Ideas: Studies on politics and philosophy before and after Marx* (London: Routledge, 1994), 61-86.

institutional forms and relations of power in which they are in-scribed, through what he termed the *ideological state appara-tuses*.[18] Through the elaboration of the concept of *ideological interpellation*, Althusser exposed how the process of the produc-tion of 'autonomous individuality', that is, the generation of the sense of self and the (mis)recognition of the self as the source of 'autonomous' agency and cognition is involved in the reproduc-tion of hegemonic ideology, that is, the reproduction of relations of domination.

Althusser's conceptualisation of the way that ideological interpellation 'works' through *ideological state apparatuses* cap-tures perfectly the set of interventions into the form and content of 'institutional behaviour' in the Croatian context which pro-vided the material grounds through which this 'internal boundary' was being reproduced. We can only enumerate here a number of the most prominent examples, for the minutiae of instances and levels at which such machinery is put to work demands an ex-tended sociological gaze. It is perhaps most interesting to look at the anxiety with which the cultural policy of the Croatian state was concerned with the production of what Balibar called *fictive ethnicity*[19] — the eruption of distasteful 'differential dictionaries' which had the function to extricate the Croatian language from the previous idiom of Serbo-Croatian (or Croato-Serbian), and to

---

[18] See 'Ideology and Ideological State Apparatuses', in Louis Althusser, *Lenin and Philosophy and Other Essays*, (London: New Left Books, 1971). For an illumi-nating re-conceptualisation of the original thesis by one of his former students see Pêcheux, 97-132. Of the most prominent contemporary discussions on Al-thusser's concept of interpellation are, Slavoj Žižek, *The Sublime Object of Ide-ology* (London: Verso, 1989); Judith Butler, *The Psychic Life of Power* (Stanford: Stanford University Press, 1997); Rastko Močnik, *3 teorije: Ideologija, nacija, institucija (3 Theories: Ideology, Nation, Institution)*, (Ljubljana: Založba /*cf., 1999).

[19] Balibar regards 'ethnicity,' in the modern usage of the term, a fabrication of the modern (nation)state, which however, is an indispensable one. As a complex of institutional sites, symbolic references and imaginary projections, fictive ethnicity produces and maintains the illusion of 'unity' 'origin' and 'identity'; that is, it constitutes a 'community' out of the heterogeneity of the population included in the nation-states. See Étienne Balibar, 'The Nation Form: History and Ideology' in Étienne Balibar and Immanuel Wallerstein, *Race, Nation, Class: Ambiguous Identities* (London: Verso, 1991), 86-106.

enforce the pedagogy of such separation; then the isolation of the 'national literary cannon' which consigned to the 'dustbin of Otherness' — and to the basements of libraries — not only the entire range of literary works produced south of Sava or east of Danube, but also the *oeuvre* of the intellectual and artistic protagonists of the anti-fascist struggle and the socialist revolution in Croatia; and not to forget the colossal efforts of historiography which Hobsbawm and Ranger described as the *invention of tradition*,[20] ranging from the significant transformations in the educational curriculae with the production of a set of 'ethnically correct' textbooks, to those embarrassing attempts whereby historiographic research was aimed to prove the 'non-Slavic origin of Croats'.

To this we should also add all the discriminatory practices inscribed in other 'official' institutional sites — the removal of Serbs from a number of public functions, the refusals to grant the new citizenship documents, confiscation of property — but also those 'amnestied' cases of the brutal use of physical force — intimidations, beatings and even murder of Serb individuals and families. At the same time, one could read the effectiveness of the new hegemonic ideology and the political demarcations which it brought about in the lingering absence of critical public, intellectual or political engagement with 'structural violence' following the state-building project in Croatia. In fact, apart from being mesmerised by the allure of the ideology of the 'transition', the public sphere in Croatia exhibited numerous signs of fascisation — traceable in the increasing appearance of prejudices and hate speech, but also in the dissemination of a demonised representation of Serbs.[21] In this sense, the most crucial moments in the building of the antagonism between the Croatian state and the

---

[20] See Eric Hobsbawm and Terrence Ranger, eds. *The Invention of Tradition* (Cambridge: Cambridge University Press, 1983).

[21] For a portrait of the processes through which the public spheres in Croatia and Serbia became saturated with nationalist, chauvinist and racist rhetoric see the analyses gathered in Skopljanac-Brunner et al. Media and War, (Zagreb: Centre for transition and civil society research, 2000). The striking thing is, of course, the analogy and the reciprocity between the extremist discourses in both of the post-Yugoslav spaces.

leadership of Croatian Serbs are not to be found on the terrain of *Realpolitik* — in the conflicting political strategies of both sides and the catastrophic decisions that they spawned — but rather in the transformation and transposition of the conflict, in the ways in which it was extended throughout the capillary networks of the society, vivid in the new modes of organisation of the institutional apparatuses and embedded in the contexts of everyday life, all until it came to be experienced as the Fichtean 'internal boundary'.

Out of many symbolic articulations, myths and imaginary projections invested in the (re)production of this mode of subjectivation, one is of particular importance for this discussion. We should bear in mind that in order for the new symbolic line of demarcation to be politically effective it had to figure as an expression of a widespread consensus around the most general political concerns and aims that all the members of the political community, by their very belonging to the political community, share — the 'consensus' around the terrain on which politics takes place. And as we emphasised before, this space was provided in its entirety by the rhetoric of the 'rebirth of history' and the 'democratic revolutions', together with the negative projection of the phantasmatic Other — 'communist totalitarianism'. The magnetism of this negative reference point was such that the new regime managed to simply transpose the conflict with the Croatian Serbs and the nationalist regime in Serbia through this binary opposition, to metaphorically condense the anti-Communist rhetoric with nationalist resentment. This is why it was 'democracy' which was seen as under threat, for the Croatian Serbs who were rejecting the contours of the new political and institutional order, while trying militantly to defend the 'old' rights and privileges that they enjoyed in the socialist system, represented heterogeneous elements on the terrain of 'democratic' politics as such. This negative representation was even more effective in light of the fact that it reverberated through the entire conflict over the legacy of the Yugoslav socialist federation; it reflected the clash between the Croatian and Slovene demands for independence and confederate reorganisation, and the politics of the Serbian nationalist leadership, its plans for a centralised federation and the 'rectification of borders' under the principle of national sovereignty. In this sense, we can say that the work of hegemonic ideology, in the Croatian context at the beginning of the nineties was not only to push 'cultural' concerns over political aims, but also to set limits to politics as such — to declare that the boundaries of 'culture' coincide with the boundaries of politics.

In order to extend the understanding of this situation and the socio-symbolic schism supporting it we should introduce another concept from Laclau's inventory: *social antagonism*.[22] Laclau's logical deduction of the antagonistic relation provokes us to look at the conflict between the Croatian state and the militant leadership of Croatian Serbs, and its violent escalation, not merely at the level of opposing political agendas or rationally articulated interests of political actors, but in terms of the antagonism between two mutually exclusive hegemonic discourses and their according modes of subjectivation — each negating the possibility of the other; but which are, nevertheless, both dependent on the reciprocal antagonistic projections for their very own integrity. The important thing to note is that what is at stake here is not a relation between two fully constituted beings — which could, in this case, denote the empirically definable or 'objectively existing' social groups or political actors — that are opposing or contradicting each other, but an impossible relation between two subjects whereby the presence of the 'Other' is experienced as the subversion and the prevention of the 'self'.[23] However, as Laclau's

---

[22] For the initial development of the concept see Ernesto Laclau and Chantal Mouffe, *Hegemony and Socialist Strategy* (London: Verso, 1985). For a further elaboration around certain deconstructionist notions see Ernesto Laclau, *New Reflections on the Revolution of Our Times* (London: Verso, 1990). For a critical assessment of the concept and an attempt of its re-elaboration by the means of Lacanian psychoanalysis, see Slavoj Žižek, 'Beyond Discourse Analysis', in Laclau, 249-260.

[23] Laclau illustrates his concept by calling upon a tragic episode from the history of social dissent: "an extreme example of [antagonism] can be found in millenarian movements. Here the world divides, through a system of paratactical equivalences, into two camps: peasant culture representing the identity of the movement, and urban culture incarnating evil. The second is the negative reverse of the first. A maximum separation has been reached: no element in the system of equivalences enters into relations other than those of opposition to the elements of the other system. There are not one but two societies. And when the millenar-

deduction remarkably shows, this very antagonistic negation, the threat represented by the 'Other', is necessary and indispensable for the subject's self-constitution — or, in this case, for the establishment of the hegemonic political order. An antagonistic force represents the 'outside' which is constitutive, as it delineates the boundaries of the self and thus at the same time affirms it. In this way we are touching upon the dimension of social and political relations that can be named the 'unconscious' — the experience of negativity which paradoxically, not only show the limits of every social objectivity or the impossibility of the constitution of a social whole without a surplus, but which is at the same time the condition of its possibility because it is only around the antagonistic negation that the socio-symbolic order can be structured at the first place.

In relation to our discussion, the important thing that we can deduce from the concept of *antagonism* is that the conflict in question wasn't merely a conflict between two modes of 'consciousness', but the 'unconscious' fact that it was only through a radical negation of the reality of the 'Other' that both of these programmes could achieve their consistency and be socially and politically effective. We are thus left with the paradox that the Croatian Serbs were not simply heterogeneous to the establishment of the new political order, but were at the same time necessary for its constitution. Only by the establishment of two mutually exclusive social realms, by the drawing of a severe social boundary and by a removal of the excessive Serbian element could the Croatian nationalists make effective their proclamation of the 'spiritual and political unity of Croats' and thus to impose the new metaphor of social totality, transcending the material contradictions and arrays of social and political differences. In other words, the hegemonic discourse could succeed in its task of 'universal representation' only through the xenophobic projection

---

ian rebellion takes place, the assault on the city is fierce, total and indiscriminate: there exist no discourses capable of establishing differences within an equivalential chain in which each and every one of its elements symbolizes evil" (Laclau and Mouffe, 130).

of Croatian Serbs who were represented as the threat to the integrity of the new body politic understood as a 'national community' — a projection that was retroactively making possible the materialisation of this myth of unity.

This constitutive nature of the denial of the reality of the antagonistic 'Other' is apparent precisely in the collision between the claims for political autonomy of both parties involved. The proclamation of the sovereignty of the Croatian state in relation to the Yugoslav context could only be made by rendering illegal and illegitimate the same secessionist demand made by Croatian Serbs who refused to be a part of this new political reality, the paradox being that both were calling upon the same universalist principle, inscribed in international legal norms as well as the Yugoslav constitutions — 'the right to national self-determination'. In fact, the two claims were thoroughly symmetrical — both pursued an ambiguous and even contradictory relationship to the Yugoslav legal and ideological underpinnings, which they recognised and negated at the same time. In the first place, both called upon the AVNOJ documents which founded the Yugoslav order on Leninist principles of 'national self-determination'. But at the same time both defined the peoplehood that was at stake in their programmes by reference to an organic metaphor. Furthermore, they linked claims to national sovereignty directly to questions of state institutions, especially those of territory. In such ways both programmes contradicted the AVNOJ principles which defined peoplehood politically, in terms of the revolutionary unity constructed in the course of the antifascist struggle, as well as the consecutive Yugoslav constitutions which recognised multiple layers of authority and sovereignty, beyond and 'beneath' the state.

*   *   *

What are the conclusions to be drawn from these ironical movements in the idiom of 'democracy'? Firstly, we would like to argue against those attempts that conceptually (and ideologically) reduce the complexity of this historical and political situation. As we have attempted to show, the nationalist ideology that was at work in the Croatian context in the early nineties did not act in a one-dimensional manner, that is, it did not impose itself in the sense of a homogeneous *Weltanschauung,* an exclusive and hermetically sealed doctrine. Rather, we should read the effectiveness of the nationalist discourses precisely in their ability to incorporate different ideological elements, to encapsulate various political demands. The strength of the nationalism proceeded from its ability to play a transversal function — to articulate a series of links between different political projects and social positions, and to impose its power over such an articulation. One of the crucial moments here was the articulation of the democratic institutions and the ideology of 'democratic revolutions' with the question of 'national sovereignty' and the political project of secession from Yugoslavia.

What does this ideological displacement of 'democracy' imply? One shouldn't simply discard the democratic ideology in this case as a kind of 'false consciousness', as a pure manipulative or demagogical device, an appearance whose truth lies somewhere else — in the 'reality' of the interests of power of the political elites, for example. Surely, there is a certain mystification involved here, because the universalist discourses of democracy are masking a political particularism, a nationalist claim made on behalf of 'culture'. But this does not mean that 'democracy' is simply a passive element in the picture, a pure 'fiction', a mere surplus expression of a 'deeper' determination. Quite the contrary, 'democracy' is the very ideological form, as well as the practical-institutional complex through which nationalist politics is played out. It is an active 'fiction' with concrete effects, a representation that is able to condense a series of tensions, political struggles and contradictions, both 'internal' and 'external' to the situation of Croatia and Yugoslavia. Its fundamental role is that it generates a social and political tie in the Gramscian sense — the social compromise necessary for the establishment and the reproduction of the new order.

What further proceeds from this is the inference that it is misleading to hastily impose an attribute of 'irrationality' to the political and ideological developments in Croatia in times of the crisis of the Yugoslav socialist context. It is obviously misleading and it can even be dangerously flawed to magnify the 'magic' of the nationalist demagogy or the uncanny charisma of the nationalist leader, to seek explanations on dubious conceptual terrains, such as those that speak about the 'irrationality' of the masses, or even worse, those that attempt to essentialise the xenophobic experience and violence by the means of a 'universalist' or a 'particularist' conception of man. In fact, Tuđman's political programme, together with the political programmes of other (post)Yugoslav national leaders, from Slovenia to Serbia, from Macedonia to Kosovo, was oriented around a specific 'rational' kernel — around the idea of the state encircled by the logic of national sovereignty and the principles of 'self—determination' — and was carried out by setting up a number of 'rational' juridico-political institutions, such as 'popular sovereignty', representative parliamentary democracy and even the institutions of 'direct democracy' (e.g. referenda), which appealed to both the 'domestic' and 'foreign' public.

But does this not also imply casting a shadow of doubt on the old dogma, mostly pronounced in the liberal tradition, about two different types of nationalism — the 'good' (inclusive, democratic, patriotic and civic) nationalism and the 'bad' (exclusive, chauvinist, ethnic or cultural) nationalism? In relation to the developments in Croatia and the ambiguous role of the empty signifier 'democracy', it is clear that such an unequivocal line cannot be drawn so easily. Contrary to the most common interpretations, we cannot simply read the project of 'Tuđmanism' with its 'archaic' and 'romantic' restoration of the ethnonationalist idea, the idea of *Kulturnation,* as the sheer Otherness of the political and democratic idea of the nation. The hegemonic project at work in Croatia at the beginning of the nineties was not a radical opposite to democratic institutions and ideology — figures of citizenship, universal suffrage, sovereign law — but was, in fact, practising this ideology and expressing itself through such institutions. The 'distance' at which the nationalist agenda was uttered here, its appeal to universalist principles and institutions is its very constitutive ground.

And yet how are we to grasp the perverse leap occurring here, the ironical motion behind the proclamations of 'democracy'? Should we interpret the surplus attached to the nationalist projects in Yugoslavia, the excess of subjective violence following their programmes — in the case of Croatia, the drive towards the expulsion of the paradoxical Serbian element, the antagonistic projection at work during the course of and through the establishment of the democratic political order — as a historical aberration? An instructive way to approach this problem could perhaps lie in certain remarks that Étienne Balibar made in relation to modern political universality. Balibar's primary observation is that the question of the appearance of violence surrounding different historical realisations of nationalism — the excessive situations of xenophobia, stigmatisation and discrimination in which various 'minority' groups are attacked by means ranging from banal acts of violence to 'ethnic cleansing' and systematic genocide — is a question of degree, a question of 'how much'. In his discussion on the relationship between nationalism and racism, he persuasively argues how the two should be seen as necessarily intertwined for they always appear together in history — the racist excess figures as a compulsory companion to different historical projects of nationalism, emerging not only alongside the processes of the formation of core European nation-states and the expansion of their might, but also following their tragic historical opposites — various anti-imperialist struggles and national liberation movements.[24] The crucial point, according to Balibar, is that racism always figures as a supplement, although an excessive supplement to nationalism. It helps to correct the lack of particularity of the latter, to provide a lasting 'substance' to the community that nationalism attempts to constitute over a contradictory social and historical reality.[25] However, Balibar additionally warns

---

[24] See 'Racism and Nationalism' in Balibar and Wallerstein, 37-68.

[25] As Balibar argues, it is the racial phantasm of 'origin', the idealisation of kinship relations and the myth of 'ancestry', of a pure substance, whether biological (blood or somatic features) or cognitive (spirit or character), being transmitted from one generation to the next, which 'corrects' the lack of particularity of each historical 'nation', giving body to the political category of the 'people' and thus overdetermining the 'unity' and the 'specificity' of the nationally constituted community. He also stresses that, as history teaches us, the backlash of this devilish covenant is such that the racist logic of purity can subvert the very positivity of the nationalist project, whereby the longing for the 'authentic racial-national

us that contrary to some of our established perceptions racism also serves nationalism as a corrective of universality, for it provides each historical nation, or more exactly each project of interpellation of individuals as national subjects, with the ideal projection of 'human nature' according to which national belonging is naturalised and elevated to a supreme role.

The structural contradiction that Balibar detects, the potentiality of violence surrounding nationalism as a modern political force, and thus also traversing its most definite political form — that of the secular nation-state, in all of its historical manifestations, even the most democratic and egalitarian ones — offer us a sobering reminder of the more general stakes underlying the concerns around the 'Yugoslav tragedy', and thus of the specific developments in Croatia that we touched upon. This particular thesis, together with the forceful problematisation of the ambiguous nature of the modern democratic subject in some prominent theoretical debates of the day,[26] does not in any way exhaust the set of structural and historical entanglements that envelop the Yugoslav post-socialist context, nor can it explain the specific brutality of this context, in terms of accounting for a set of historical and political circumstances which brought about an alarming saturation with fascistoid elements in these local nationalisms, but it does seem to offer a productive way to move forward. If nothing, it helps us to overcome the narcissistic fixation on the personalities and the 'ethnographies' of our particular histories. In this sense, our general remark would be that rather than looking at the excesses of the nationalist ideologies in the Yugoslav context and the outbursts of violence, both banal and systematic, that they brought about, as a form of pathology, especially as an anomaly in relation to the prophecies of the historical transformations in the (post)socialist East at the end of the nineteen eighties

---

community' witnesses its inverted form — the stigmatisation of the 'impure' elements (groups, individuals, customs), and its externalisation through the violent attempts to cleanse the 'national body' by the exclusion or extermination of 'false' elements. Ibid.

[26] See Étienne Balibar, *Politics and the Other Scene* (London: Verso, 2002); Jacques Rancière, *On the Shores of Politics* (London: Verso, 1995); Alain Badiou, *Abrégé de métapolitique* (Paris: Seuil, 1998).

— the so-called 'democratic revolutions' — we should try to understand them as internal moments of a wider structure, or of a structural transformation that is. Of course, this is far from proposing that what was at play here was the historical teleology of certain 'archaic resurrections', of 'unresolved aspirations' or 'lingering particularisms' subdued and suppressed for centuries, or rather, in the second part of the twentieth century, which finally sought their resolution with the collapse of the system keeping them captive, and did so even more violently because of its alleged 'totalitarian nature'. Obviously, we do need to account for a set of particular historical conditions, such as the complex structure of the Yugoslav socialist society and the reservoir of political and ideological traditions stretching out beyond and beneath Tito's Yugoslavia. But the real questions, in our view, have to be directed towards the specificity of the general historical moment in which ideological and political 'archaisms' (re)emerge as problems or agendas. The paradox to be addressed is the re-emergence of the nationalist ideology in the age in which the idea of consensus dominates, of the hegemony of the universalist discourses of pacification (such as human rights or multiculturalism). In a different but nonetheless interconnected sense, it is also the paradox of the 'resurrection' of the desire towards the nation-form in a global social context characterised by the crisis of such form, with the hypertrophy of transnational flows of capital, universalising cultural products and supra-national political institutions.

Ozren Pupovac *is a member of the Department of Sociology, The Open University, Milton Keynes, United Kingdom.*

Desecularizing Secularism: Post-secular history, non-juridical justice, & active forgetting

Ananda Abeyesekere

Death of God and Secularist Complacency

Nietzsche tells us in his *Gay Science* that one day, early in the bright morning, a madman arrived in a market with a lantern and jumped into [people's] midst and pierced them with his eyes. "'Whither is God?' he cried; 'I will tell you, *we have killed him*— you and I. ...God is dead. God remains dead. And we have killed him." Following this pronouncement, the madman poses a series of rhetorical questions about the event—from how it became possible for God to be killed to what might be invented to replace Him. He then yells at the silent, bewildered crowd: "I have come too early... My time is not yet. This tremendous event is still on its way, still wandering: It has not yet reached the ears of men. Lightening and thunder require time. The light of the stars requires time. Deeds, though done, still require time to be seen and heard. The deed is still more distant from them than the most distant stars—*and yet they have done it themselves.*"[1]

These are arguably some of the most evocative, elusive, and—if one can say this about a master of suspicion—corrosive words that *seemingly* represent one of Nietzsche's devastating attacks on the edifice of (Christian) religion, morality, and civilization sustained by European modernity.[2] Now, if these Nietzschean

---

[1] Frederich Nietzsche, *The Gay Science* (New York: Vintage, 1974), sec 123.

[2] For samples of the continuing academic interests in the questions about the "Death of God," see Robert B. Pippin, "Nietzsche and the Melancholy of Modernity," *Social Research* 66, no. 2 (1999) Michael Harr, "Nietzsche and the Metamorphosis of the Divine," in *Post-Secular Philosophy: Between Philosophy and Theology,* ed. Phillip Blond (New York: Routledge, 1988), 158-164. Tyler T. Roberts, *Contesting Spirit: Nietzsche, Affirmation, and Religion* (Princeton: Princeton University Press, 1998), 196-98. Louis A. Ruprecht, Jr, "Nietzsche, the

words constitute as self-evident a critique of religion as they may appear at first sight, then it seems difficult, if not impossible, to pass through Nietzsche to arrive at the task of desecularizing secularism. In other words, Nietzsche's critique, it seems, endorses readily the secularist, Enlightenment claims about the de-divinized public spaces of rational argument that liberal thinkers ranging from Kant to Rorty and Rawls (in their own varying ways) have considered so essential to our modernity and its attendant virtues of tolerance, pluralism, and democracy.[3]

Nietzsche, of course, remained far less sanguine about the possibility that we would come to know, much less fathom the gravity of, the death of God so soon. He suspected that it would take "thousands of years" before we would come to know it since the "shadow" of God would continue to appear in different guises. Viewing from a comparativist angle, Nietzsche claimed that "After the Buddha was dead, his shadow was still shown for centuries in a cave—a tremendous, gruesome shadow. God is Dead; but given the way of men, there may still be caves for thousands of years in which his shadow will be shown.—And—we—we still have to vanquish this shadow, too" (*Gay Science,* sec. 108). Nietzsche, however, suspected that the shadow of this recent "greatest event," that is, the idea that "the belief in God has become unbelievable" was already beginning to hover over Europe, and with the dawn of the "breakdown, ruin, destruction, and cataclysm" of this belief, a new horizon "appears free to us again, if it should not be bright... The sea, *our* sea, lies open again; perhaps there has never been such an open sea" (*Gay Science,* sec. 343).

The idea of the "shadow" of God constitutes, as I read it, a strategic move on Nietzsche's part. On the one hand, it cautions against the lapse into complacency about the secularism of political modernity. On the other, it forestalls the most obvious em-

Death of God, and Truth, or Why I Still Like Reading Nietzsche," *Journal of the American Academy of Religion* 65, no. 3 (1997): 573-586.

[3] Literature on this is abundant. My own take on Kant and Rorty is found in Abeysekara, "Identity for and against Itself." *Journal of the American Academy of Religion* (forthcoming).

pirico-epistemological question: if God is dead, how and why does "religion" (Christianity) still operate as a visible discourse/practice in many parts of the world? Now some defenders of secularism would rush to warn us that this question is no longer worth asking today. This is because, they would argue, compared to the ways in which it was once visible a century or so ago, Christianity has lost its grip of power, prestige, and influence on the "first world." This is precisely the kind of argument that British sociologist Steven Bruce advances in his latest book, aptly titled *God is Dead*.[4] Curiously lacking any reference to Nietzsche, yet illustrated by a front-page picture of a church converted—if this is the right word—to Mike's Carpet Stores: Discount Warehouse in West Yorkshire, England, *God is Dead* is a post-Weberian confirmation, if not a celebration, of secularism's disenchantment with and indeed its gradual triumph over religion in the West. In this story of triumph, secularism comes to stand as a synonym for the decline in religion. By reference to a sociological archive of statistical data—from decrease in church membership and Sunday School attendance to what he calls the "Easternization of the West"—Bruce would have us believe "that the declining social significance of [Christian] religion causes a decline in the number of religious people and the extent to which they are religious." Differentiating his version from conventional notions, secularism, Bruce contends, is not so much caused by science as by a certain kind of "indifference." As he elucidates, "Most people did not give up being committed Christians because they became convinced that religion was *false*. It simply ceased to be of great importance to them; they became indifferent" (235). Bruce's is not an isolated argument. Charles Taylor, who might resist being labeled a secularist, seems to buy readily into Bruce's statistical claim, if not the secularist complacency embedded in it, when he cites the latter's previous work: "The immeasurable, external results of [a post-war slide into a 'fractured culture'] are as we might expect: first a rise in those who state themselves to be atheists, agnostics, or to have no religion in many countries. But be-

---

[4] Steven Bruce, *God is Dead: Secularization in the West* (London: Blackwell, 2002).

yond this the gamut of intermediate positions widens: many people drop out of active practice, while still declaring themselves as
belonging in God. On another dimension, the gamut of the beliefs
in something beyond widens, with fewer declaring belief in a personal God while more hold to something like an impersonal
force; in other words, wider range of people express religious beliefs that move outside Christian orthodoxy."[5]

For Bruce, then, and perhaps for Taylor, the former
church-cum-discount-carpet warehouse is an indubitable signifier
of that indifference. Steeped in an academic tradition of objectivity in which sociologists "describe and explain" but do not "regret
or rejoice," Bruce seems at best content with the emergence of this
indifference to religion. Nietzsche, of course, would have railed
against this self-satisfaction as premature and indeed unworthy of
our political modernity because it might hinder the possibility of
self-fashioning or fashioning "ourselves" that he considered crucial to the politics of freedom. Nietzsche questions this sort of
complacency in *The Gay Science*: "I do not see how we could remain content with such buildings [abandoned churches] even if
they were stripped of their churchly purposes. The language spoken by these buildings is far too rhetorical and unfree, reminding
us that they are houses of God and monuments of some supra-
mundane intercourse; we who are godless could not think *our
thoughts* in such surroundings." We could not remain content,
Nietzsche argues, until our "godless" selves would become permanent parts of such buildings stripped of churchly purposes. We
could not remain content, he avers in the most ironic sense, until
we would "see *ourselves* translated into stone and plants [of such
buildings]." We could not remain content until we would "take
walks *in ourselves* when we stroll around these buildings and
[their] gardens" (*Gay Science*, sec. 280). This Nietzschean refusal
to remain content until we "could see ourselves translated into
stone and plants" and until we would "take walks *in ourselves*"
points to the kind of critical suspicion that we ought to cultivate
concerning the available demarcation between religion and secu-

---

[5] Charles Taylor, *Varieties of Religion Today: William James Revisited* (Harvard: Harvard University Press, 2002), 106-107.

larism or between what Nietzsche called "church and [public] life."

The Enemy/Adversary Within

Even though Nietzsche claims (in *Twilight of the Idols*) that "church is *inimical* to life,"[6] his metaphorical, indeed almost comical vision of inserting our godless selves into the very being of the church does not permit the comfortable political distance that modern secularists labor to maintain from religion. In other words, here Nietzsche wants to dislodge us from the self-secured zones of political comfort and complacency about a transparent understanding of the parameters of our secular world and religion, church and public life. If we take, in the most metaphorical sense, "church" for the Christian "religion" Nietzsche considers his archenemy, (most clearly in *Anti-Christ*), the idea of translating "ourselves" into stones of the church alludes to the possibility of imagining a new kind of political relation between such seemingly opposed political categories as friend and enemy, and by extension, self and other, public and private. It is perhaps through reimagining this relation between enemy and friend that the emergence of the Nietzschean "overman" becomes possible, that is, the type of being/belonging antithetical to "'modern' men, to 'good' men, to Christians and other nihilists" (*Ecce Homo* III I; cited in *Twilight*, 105).

This is Nietzsche at his affirmative best. Antithetical though it is to modernity and Christianity, the identity of the "overman"—this is crucial to note—is not one that wallows in the simple negation of such concepts as goodness, belief, and truth. Rather, the identity of the "overman" is one of affirmation, affirmation of a kind of being that is "beyond good and evil." The "overman," in other words, embodies the possibility of godless selves, those "who do not readily deny" but seek "honor in being *affirmative*" (*Twilight*, V6). Understood in broad terms, this Nietzschean practice of affirming the kind of being and belonging

---

[6] Nietzche, *Twilight of the Idols or How to Philosophize With a Hammer*, trans. Duncun Large (New York: Oxford University Press, 1998), 21.

opposed to the "good men" and "modern men" cannot simply be cultivated by the comfort of distance and dissonance between enemy and friend, religion and secularism now available to our political disposal. That practice can come from the cultivation of a post-secular discomfort of forging a new relation between religion and secularism, that is, —if I may push the idea a bit further—by conceiving of a politics that would oblige us to honor the non-secular "enemy within" the domain of secular politics (*Twilight*, 55).[7]

It is through the politics of a new alliance between friend and enemy, between "godless" selves and "godly" men, that the practice of taking "walks in ourselves" can, *perhaps,* see the light of day. In the sort of new alliance I have in mind, the identity of the enemy can become reconfigured. Now, "enemy," as Foucault has reminded us, is not a helpful political category. An enemy is born out of polemics, not out of "politics." The difference between polemics and politics is that the former "establishes the other as an enemy, an upholder of opposed interests against which one must fight until the moment this enemy is defeated and either surrenders or disappears."[8] Here it is instructive to heed Foucault's argument. For Foucault polemics is "nothing more than theater." The "reactivations" that polemics generate are similar to the histrionics characteristic of a theater. In polemics/theater, he claims, "one gesticulates: anathemas, excommunications, condemnations, battles, victories, and defeats are no more than ways of speaking, after all" (*Polemics,* 112-113). Foucault goes on to ask, "Has anyone seen a new idea come out of a polemic? And how could it be otherwise, given that here the interlocutors are incited not to advance, not to take more and more risks in what they say, but to fall back continually on the rights that they claim, on their legitimacy, which they must defend, and on the affirmation of their innocence" (ibid.). Note that what is being urged by Foucault here is the possibility of a practice of politics in which

---

[7] Michel Foucault, "Subject and Power.," in *Power: Essential Works of Foucault 1954-1984*, ed. James Faubion (New York: Free Press, 1984), 326-348.
[8] Michel Foucault, "Politics, Polemics, and Problematization," in *Ethics, Subjectivity, and Truth*, ed., Paul Rabinow (The Free Press: New York, 1997), 112.

the enemy must cease to be the enemy as such. In such a politics, the enemy is not to be either annihilated or tolerated. Now it is important to stress that such a politics does not necessarily abandon incitement or provocation. Indeed the enemy becomes—again to borrow a phrase from Foucault— a certain kind of adversary worth the political investment of a "permanent provocation." But it is a politics of provocation in which competing interlocutors— moralists and secularists, "fundamentalists" and atheists, nationalists and centrists—do not merely dismiss each other because of their a priori ethical convictions. Rather it is a politics in which they provoke and incite each other to take "risks in what they say" in a public sphere, with no recourse to *merely* defending the "rights" of what is being said.

My point here that the secularist defense of history is akin to a defense of rights. As we will see soon, secularists have a certain history, and so long as they appeal to the virtue of that history, they can never take the kind of political risks crucial to fashioning new vistas of politics. They can only defend the rights of their historicist claims—however varying they may be—about secularism against their political enemies and critics. They can only fall back on the affirmation of their innocence because the epistemological grounds on which they engage their opponents are already familiar and hence safe. But, as I will show later, resorting to historicist claims and arguments can produce only a dead end of political despair. What I propose is a path out of this dead end. This involves giving up certain claims to the kind of history in which secularism remains anchored. In this light, desecularizing secularism is essentially a task of dehistoricizing history. We need a strategy that will help us understand Nietzsche's idea of active forgetting of history vis-à-vis Derrida's meditation on Hamlet's overture of "time is out of joint." This can help us desecularize secularism and think anew about justice, which, as Derrida claims, should be irreducible to any "law or rights".[9] This is because the secularist defense of history is a tacit defense of law. Once this option of resorting to law is unavailable,

---

[9] Derrida, *The Spectres of Marx: The State of the Debt, The Work of Mourning, and the New International* (New York: Routledge, 1995), xix-xx.

we can think of justice in a non-juridical way that sets aside the well-known Rawlsian notion of "justice as fairness." [10] Desecularizing secularism, as will be explained later, cannot even be attempted as long as the complacency of the ilk mentioned dominates the contemporary thinking on secularism.

The Crisis of Secularism

The politics of complacency about secularism/secularization that Steven Bruce's *God is Dead* offers us does not question the self-evident nature of the boundary between religion and secularism much less imagine new domains of politics. This much should be obvious by now. But there remains a more serious problem that is not so readily apparent in *God is Dead*. The text's complacency about our secular present—understood in terms of that progressive "indifference" to religion— amounts to rehashing the dated dictum of the "West-is-secular" that rolls off the tongues of many liberals and secularists these days. In this regard, Bruce's *God is dead* is implicated in a broader problematic of the enduring western production and canonization of the nexus of power/knowledge about post-secular demarcations between identity and difference. Here I imagine some (anti-essentialists) already registering complaints to the effect that not all liberals claim that the West is secular or that liberalism cannot be equated with secularism. As should be evident later, these sorts of complaints remain misdirected in light of the complex deployment of the West-is-secular discourse. The dictum is no longer one that liberals alone employ; it is one that even critics of secularism or "born-again Christians" use—albeit with a slightly different spin on it—in the name of democracy today, and it is undergirded by a certain logic of the "liberal" notion of tolerance. To put it quite bluntly, this problematic, it seems to me, threatens to put those liberal secularists, whose political careers have been staked on an exclusivist claim to the domain of secularism and tolerance, out of business. This is perhaps what Talal Asad has in mind when he

---

[10] John Rawls, *A Theory of Justice* (Cambridge: Harvard University Press, 1971 [2000]).

notes that "liberals are generally dismayed at the resurgence of the right, but the notion of primordial intolerance will not explain it."[11] Put differently, if the West-is-secular discourse is ceasing to be the ideological commodity of the secularists and atheists, we will have to confront the present urgency of rethinking and desecularizing secularism.

Something of this urgency may be recognized in light of the brief speech that President George W. Bush gave during his nationally televised visit to the Islamic Center of Washington D.C., six days after 9-11. Bush's seven-minute speech was supposed to allay the fears of American Muslims who had been threatened, attacked, shot at, and killed by some white Americans in different parts of the country. Among some two hundred reported cases of the attacked and murdered were non-Muslim South Asians "mistaken" to be Muslims of Arabic descent. Bush's attempt to allay the Muslims' fears was simultaneously an attempt to allay the suspicions of his "fellow [non-Muslim-white-Christian] Americans" about *the* identity of Islam and Muslims. To do so, Bush drew a distinction between the suspected Muslim "evil-doers" who masterminded the 9-11 attacks and ordinary Muslims. That is, he made a distinction between "true" Muslims and terrorists who call themselves "Muslims." "These acts of violence against innocents," the President claimed, "violate the fundamental tenets of the Islamic faith. And it's important for my fellow Americans to understand that." Perhaps the most profound moment of his visit to the mosque was the moment when the President, flanked by a few American Muslim men and women, held up a copy of the Koran and asserted: "The face of terror is not the true faith of Islam. That's not what Islam is all about. Islam is peace. These terrorists don't represent peace. They represent evil and war."[12]

This moment of Bush's holding up the Koran and proclaiming that "Islam is peace" constitutes, for me, simultaneously

---

[11] Talal Asad, *The Formations of the Secular: Christianity, Islam, Modernity* (Stanford: Stanford University Press, 2002), 177.

[12] The text of Bush's speech can be found at http: //www.whitehouse.gov/ news/releases/2001/09/20010917-11.html.

a moment of the triumph of tolerance and a moment of the crisis of secularism and liberalism. It is a moment of the triumph of tolerance because it is the secular West's commitment to the practice of the "tolerance" of Others— a principle bound up with the "non-fanaticism" of the West—that presumably made it possible for George W. Bush, a self-proclaimed admirer of Jesus as the "best philosopher," to visit a Muslim house of worship and cite a passage from the Koran. As I watched Bush make these remarks on television, I wondered if one could, in some weird way, think of it as bearing some semblance to the ethnographic practice of "participant observation" that has defined and sustained the unstable proximity among the West, anthropology, and its constructed native others. Unlike a typical anthropologist, Bush, of course, did more than simply participate/observe; he *intervened*. He did so, not as an insider, but as a *tolerant* outsider, to insist that "Islam is peace." One cannot imagine anti-essentialist postcolonial critics and anthropologists ever advocating this kind of moral (indeed state) intervention in questions of what and who constitute the parameters of "(an)other's "true" religious identity. Such intervention, they might claim (perhaps rightly so), essentializes another's tradition, robbing it of its own voices. Today better informed postcolonial anti-essentialists might easily ridicule and discount Bush's intervention at the Islamic Center as a machination of a pretentious, not to mention right-wing, politician hardly familiar with the Koran or the nuances of the Arabic language to claim that the English translation of a verse he cited is not "as eloquent as the original Arabic." However, my intention here is not to pursue such an anti-essentialist criticism. Such a criticism will accomplish nothing but a mere dismissal of that "intervention." It seems to me that we can no longer cultivate that sort of knee-jerk dismissal for the sake of deepening our critique of colonial imperialism and essentialism and celebrating the agency of colonized native religions and cultures, without offering an alternative practice of politics. Such a summary dismissal would not be able to understand how the kind of tolerance that marked the Bush visit to the Islamic Center produces a profound ethical problem that signals the crisis, if not the failure, of liberalism.

If a certain (post-Tocquevillean?) tradition of democratic tolerance enabled Bush to inform/remind non-Muslim Americans of Islam as a religion of peace, that tolerance became possible at a costly price. On the one hand, if that tolerance sought to extend to Muslims the generosity of the President's pleading for "fellow citizens to understand" and recognize what constitutes Muslim identity, it did so by making Muslims pay the price of being represented as misunderstood yet visible Arab-American "Others." The otherness of Muslims can only be comprehended by the abstract quality of "peace." On the other hand, if the possibility of this plea for the non-Muslim understanding and recognition of Muslims in America marks the triumph of tolerance, the moment of that plea marks a moment of the crisis of secular liberalism that labors to foster, but *always* is threatened by, the divergent politics of cultural and religious pluralism. Put differently, the moment in which the plea was made was the moment in which pluralism threatened the "stable" relation that the secular state strives to maintain between the nation, citizenship, and freedom. If the discourse of freedom is crucial to the apparatus of the secular nation-state, to its guaranteeing and facilitating the "free exercise" of different religious and cultural choices among its citizens in a pluralistic society, the attacks by "fellow citizens" on "Muslims" in the immediate aftermath of 9/11 undoubtedly injured that freedom. Seen in this light, the relation between freedom and pluralism becomes unstable, indeed unsustainable, because freedom does not so much make pluralism possible as that pluralism threatens the very survival of freedom. What can stabilize that unstable relation is tolerance—that is, "fellow citizens" extending tolerance towards [cultural-religious] others. Tolerance, however, cannot guarantee the lasting stability of that relation since pluralism, appearing as it does in diverse and shifting forms, will stand as a threat to freedom.

Freedom then will always have to live with the threat of pluralism, so to speak, always anticipating the injury that it may cause to freedom, since to eliminate that threat, to say no to pluralism, is to risk freedom's own demise. After all, freedom will cease to be freedom if it cannot sustain the moral space in which the "free exercise" of plural ethical and political choices of being are possible, either by the "majority" or the "minority" of a given democratic nation-state. Understood this way, then, the Rawlsian idea of giving priority to liberty/freedom over all other values and goods simply becomes untenable because freedom becomes secondary to, and often needs to be rescued by, tolerance. [13] My argument here then is this: If tolerance can never really eliminate the threat of pluralism to freedom, and if it can never really prevent "fellow citizens" from *misunderstanding* the differences of certain other citizens, the only effective strategy a state/nation can take to reduce that threat is to periodically remind citizens of the virtue of the practice of tolerance, of its significance to secular freedom, which allows the nation to distinguish itself from other non-secular (often non-western) nations supposedly lacking in that western virtue.

This reminding has a certain similarity to the West-is-secular discourse, repeated in so many redundant ways by secularists such as John Rawls on the one hand and Steven Bruce on the other. So when George W. Bush rushed to assert that "Islam is peace," he did not just ask his fellow citizens to "understand" and tolerate Muslim others because of their alleged affinity to their Christian tradition of "peace"; he *also* extolled the West's tradition of secularism and tolerance momentarily forgotten by his fellow citizens. Thus what is demanded of the fellow citizens in the plea is not necessarily respect for or understanding of Muslim others; what is demanded is certainly not the exploration of the spaces of differing Islamic practices in which "Islam" as such becomes irreducible to the homogenous notion of "Islam-is-peace," practices that can thwart the rush to define what is and is not Islam and render problematic the very ideas of *understanding* and *respecting* the otherness of Islam/Muslims that supposedly stands in opposition to "fellow citizens." Rather what is demanded here is respect for the West's own secular tradition of tolerance and the importance placed on freedom. So, for me, this plea marks a moment of the crisis of secularism not merely because it is made by a born-again Christian conservative, threatening (as he arguably

---

[13] Rawls, *A Theory of Justice*, 214-220.

does) to deprive secularists and liberals of their long-possessed privilege to make claims about secularism and tolerance; the plea marks a moment of the crisis of secularism because the politics of solution that it offers to the problem of pluralism and its perceived threat to freedom are based on the shaky principle of tolerance whose collapse can be (temporally) averted by the West-is-secular discourse. Obviously, then, the plea for tolerance can guarantee no lasting solution; it has to be made and re-made as our socio-political circumstances may shift and the fellow citizens may forget the virtue of tolerance.

Here we return full circle to the Nietzschean suspicion of secularism with which we started. If the discourses of the "West-is-secular" and "Islam-is-peace" are two sides of the same coin, and if they constitute the most effective politics of responding to the problem of cultural and religious differences and safeguarding freedom, Nietzsche's refusal to remain content with secularism (that is, if we understand his comical refusal to remain content with the former "houses" of God," stripped of their churchly purposes, as an expression of his dissatisfaction with secularism and modernity) poses a new demand for imagining alternative politics of reckoning with the cultural and religious differences in a new post-secular world.

In view of the above discussion, we can suspect now that the route of seeking to understand minority "Others" usually takes us back to the temporary refuge of tolerance. The problem with the idea of understanding a minority religion is obviously that it revolves around the messy business of sorting through empiricist-historicist questions of which embodied concepts, ideas, practices, and debates constitute the proper identity of that religion. If the task of understanding such minority religions can produce any tolerance, that tolerance cannot be anything but an act of personal or collective generosity that someone or some group might extend toward others different from them. Tolerance can be only so because it is not clear why seeking to understand—in terms of reading and thinking about—the differences of another's religion or cultural tradition would be followed by one's tolerance, if not respect, towards it. One could be easily insulted, if not threatened, by another's perceived religious and cultural differences. This was clearly evident when, in the months following 9/11, US televangelists (like John Hagee in Texas) quoted passages from the Bible, in their sermons and compared them to those from the Koran to contend that, contrary to some popular claims, Christianity and Islam are not (and would never be) "sister faiths" because Islam is not a religion of peace. Seeing this as a selective reading-understanding of Islam by a misguided fundamentalist Christian will not suffice.

Now, the demand for an alternative politics that sets aside the virtue of tolerance does not abandon secularism. Rather, locating an alternative to tolerance is a new demand for secularism. That demand is for secularism to "desecularize" itself. Desecularizing does not mean we have more or less of secularism. It means that if tolerance, marked by the discourses like the West-is-secular and Islam-is-peace, constituted the kind of politics through which secularism has sought to sustain its claims to the distinction between religion and the secular space, it needs to rethink those politics because the terms of how and by whom that distinction is maintained have radically altered. My proposal here is that secularism can do this by setting itself a new task which involves rethinking secularism's reliance on history. In a nutshell, what I wish to suggest is that secularism will have to give up some of its claims to history to sustain its claims; it has to engage in a practice of "active forgetting" of a certain sense of history. My intimation is that the kind of politics that might emerge through secularism's active forgetting of history might provide the grounds upon which that Nietzschean comical vision of taking "walks in ourselves" when we stroll around the buildings and gardens of the former houses of God, at least, becomes imaginable for ourselves.

Desecularizing Secularism, Forgetting History

To imagine the possibility of such a politics, I now turn to a debate involving those who might be called atheists, fundamentalists, and the state in contemporary America. The debate is about the question of whether the "In-God-We-Trust" motto on US currency violates the separation of church and state on the one hand and civil rights on the other. Obviously, the debate echoes general questions about the role of religion within American public life that (re)gained visibility within the public domain in the summer of 2003, particularly in the wake of the high-profiled controversy involving the 5, 280-pound granite monument displaying the Ten Commandments that Alabama's Chief Justice Roy Moore installed in the rotunda of the Alabama Supreme Court. Moore defied a court order to have it removed from the courthouse. Later, in August and November of 2003, respectively, against a modest opposition from some evangelical power brokers, Moore's own associates not only removed the monument from the rotunda (wheeled away on live television to a storage room in the courthouse) but also expelled Judge Moore himself from office. This was preceded by several other less familiar controversies about what seems, at least from the perspectives of self-described secularists or atheists, like attempts by radical Christians to insert religion into various levels of the secular space. For secularists such attempts come in terms of Christian demands for adopting class-room prayer and the phrase "under God" in the pledge of allegiance in public schools and inscribing symbols of God within other public buildings. Generally the secularists see such demands as undermining the constitutional ban on the separation of church and state while their advocates (the so called fundamentalists) view the opposition to them as efforts to deny the nation its religious "history" and heritage. (Indeed, Judge Moore flouted the court order to remove the monument claiming that the law of the land was based on the law of God.)

These sorts of disputes are usually settled through the courts, often initiated by lawsuits filed by the ACLU (American Civil Liberties Union) on behalf of the plaintiffs. The secularists see favorable rulings as affirmations of the principle of the separation of church and state required by the first amendment to the constitution, which they claim is rooted in a secular "history." The courts' interventions in upholding the constitution, deciding whether or not a given religious symbol or practice within the secular space violates the separation of church and state are themselves an interpretation and affirmation of "history," that is, adjudicating if a given public act or practice (concerning religion) of the present violates the "original" principle or precedent of the past. In this sense, for the non-violation of the original principle to exist, there must be a correspondence between the past and the present. For the secularists these juridical affirmations of history, sustaining that relation between the past and the present, that safeguards the distinction between church and state, is a self-evident form of "justice." This idea of justice is clearly embedded in the conventional understanding that "law" (the courts' inter-pretation or affirmation of the constitution/the first amendment) delivers justice. On this view, justice is to be found in history, in a historic principle, which, in this case, is the principle of the sepa-ration of church and state, enshrined in the first amendment.

What I am after in the rest of this paper is to understand if secularism can continue to think of history and justice in this way. Put differently, my interest in seeking to desecularize secularism, to understand if secularism can always have recourse to justice via history is to explore how we might find justice elsewhere, outside of history, that's to say, justice from the present, and, if you will, from the "future of the present."

The debate about the In-God-We-Trust motto on US cur-rency constitutes an ideal site for this task. It is not a debate in the sense of a legal dispute between some branch of the federal gov-ernment and secular citizens that remains pending to be settled through the intervention of a court ruling, at least not for the time being. Indeed the absence of a call for an immediate legal inter-vention to settle the questions about the supposed (un)constitutionality of the motto on the currency points to the difficulty of resorting to history/historicist claims to defend and sustain the secularist demands today. As the American atheists, arguably the most staunch defenders of secularism, explain: "Across the country, there is a movement afoot. It isn't using picket signs, or a flood of letters to Congress, or even a lawsuit— that's already been tried. Instead, some atheists and separationists are taking pen in hand and crossing out the motto 'In God We Trust' from the national currency. Others are using rubber stamps, or inserting their own messages like 'In Reason we Trust,' or 'Keep Church and State Separate.' ...Simply put, atheists do not like the

'In God We Trust' slogan staring at us every time we pull out our wallets or purses. It has to go. But how?"[14]

What is worth noting in this statement is not the obvious concession to the inefficacy, if not the failure, of the strategies that usually animate political protests—picketing, law suits, marching, etc—because they "already have been tried." But such strategies remain ineffective because they cannot combat the power of the *normalized,* and by extension, *legalized* history of the motto on the national currency. There is, in other words, an implicit admission in the above statement that the motto has become part of history, not just the history of the national currency, but the history of the United States. Put differently, the motto has become "history" itself. Unlike the recent adoption of class prayer in a public school or the installation of a religious symbol in a federal building, against which the strategies of picketing and lawsuits, might spur quick legal action, protests against the motto does not seem to do so. This is perhaps because the "unconstitutionality" of the motto remains invisible to us today, hidden by history/time. It remains hidden by time itself because, as one might say, it has been there for some time. It has become not only normalized but also legalized by time, because one can locate the time(s) when its appearance on the currency was made possible by (post-first amendment) bills/laws. Then, perhaps, the atheist admission is that the normalized and legalized status, and indeed, the identity, of the motto on the currency makes it difficult for the secularists to appeal to law to recognize the unconstitutionality of the motto. What is interesting about this appeal is that it is really a demand for law to sever law's own relation to itself since the very being of the motto on the currency now remains "legal" today. The difficulty of challenging the legality/law is clear in the following statement:

> One of the first legal actions to challenge religious sloganeering of this type was made in 1978 by American Atheists founder Madalyn Murray O'Hair. In the case of

---

[14] "In God We Trust' —Stamping out Religion on National Currency," http://www.atheists.org/flash.line/igwt1.htm

MADALYN MURRAY O'HAIR et al. v. W. MICHAEL BLUMENTHAL SECRETARY OF THE TREASURY, et al. (462 F. Supp. 19 -- W.D. Tex 1978), the court opined: "Its use is of a patriotic or ceremonial character and bears no true resemblance to a governmental sponsorship of religious exercise." The U.S. Court of Appeals for the Ninth Circuit reached a similar conclusion in the 1970 case ARONOW v. UNITED STATES. Subsequent cases also fell short, even though they argued that the motto clearly encouraged religion and made a statement about god and theology. On September 14, 1988, then-President of American Atheists Jon Murray addressed the Subcommittee on Consumer Affairs and Coinage concerning proposals to redesign the nation's currency. At that time, Murray expressed concern about including "In God We Trust" on the national currency, suggesting instead a return to the secular "E Pluribus Unum" ("One from many") that was used earlier in the nation's history (ibid.).

Now, if secularists seem to find it difficult to turn to law in the conventional way to prove the unconstitutionality of the "religious graffiti" on the currency, then they must find an option beyond law. The readily available alternative, of course, is history/time itself. But this alternative does not provide easy solutions. In turning to history, the difficult question that the secularists face is whether or not they can establish a certain temporal distance between history and the motto, that is, if they can demonstrate that the distance between the (original time of the) first amendment and the time of the appearance of the In-God-We-Trust motto on the currency is constitutionally unbridgeable. In seeking to do so, they must find a way to deny any relation between the two. Now for the secularists to negate this relation is to negate the (existing) relation between the motto and the post-first amendment law that "legalized" it. That is to say, they must show that the law that made possible the appearance of the motto on the currency is unjust because it violates the "original" time (or "original intent") of the constitution/first amendment.[15] This,

---

[15] Legal scholars have pointed to the implausibility of trying to figure out the "original intent" of documents like the constitution. In many instances, the interpretations of legislative acts may become legislative acts themselves. See Jeremy

perhaps, is the only way for them to restore the original law of the constitution/first amendment.

To accomplish this, atheists must, then, narrate the history of the original law of the separation of church and state. This is precisely what the atheists do when they ask, "Where did 'In God We Trust' originate?" Contrary to what they claim is the common public belief that the motto has been on the currency since revolutionary times, atheists set out to delineate the history of how the motto came to be adopted as the national symbol, and why it conveys today a distinctly religious message. The first national motto was "E Pluribus Unum." Thomas Jefferson first recommended it, and it was later endorsed by Benjamin Franklin; it became part of the Great Seal of the United States. All this happened just five years prior to the constitutional convention of 1787. The atheists contend that "it wasn't until a century later, though, that 'In God We Trust' was seriously proposed as a motto." Quoting Madalyn O'Hair the author of "Freedom Under Siege," they claim that the argument for the case was made in 1861 by Reverend M.R. Watkinson. Watkinson proposed to the secretary of the treasury that the motto be put on the coins because America is a "Judeo-Christian nation," and that it should recognize that "there is but one God." Supposedly swayed by the arguments of the religious community that buttressed Watkins claim, and conscious of the importance of the votes of that community, Congress passed the Coinage Act of April 22, 1864. The act authorized the inscription of the In-God-We-Trust phrase on the coins. The motto first appeared on the two-cent coin in 1864, on the one-cent coin in 1901, and it has appeared on dimes since 1916. Eventually it was imprinted on gold coins, silver dollars, and half dollar coins.

According to the atheists, the real "religionizing" of the national currency took place in 1955 under the leadership of President Dwight Eisenhower, who signed public law 140 that required the imprinting of the motto on all currency, and this completely replaced the phrase E Pluribus Unum. Here the athe-

---

Waldron, *Law and Disagreement* (New York: Oxford University Press, 1999), esp. 119-146.

ists remind us of the familiar Cold War background against which this religionizing of the currency took place.

> All of this occurred at the height of the cold war tension when the political division between the Soviet Union and the western bloc was simplistically portrayed as a confrontation between the Judeo-Christian civilization and the 'godless' menace of communism. Indeed the new national motto was only part of a broader effort effectively to religionize civic ritual and symbols. On June 14, 1954, Congress unanimously ordered the inclusion of the words 'Under God' into the Pledge of Allegiance. By this time, other laws mandating public religiosity had also been enacted, including a statute for all federal justices and judges to wear an oath concluding with 'So help me God.'

For the secularists to tell the "history" of how the In-God-We-Trust motto became part of the national currency is to tell the history of how a nation conceived in the ideals of secular governance, with no privileging of one particular religion, was religionized. As the secularists claim, the public has taken this for granted to such an extent that the religionized identity of the currency is now assumed to be part of the identity of the nation. In other words, for many in the US, "religionized" identity of the currency is a self-evident testimony to the "religious" identity of the nation. The secularists remain understandably frustrated by the public unawareness of an irony here.

> Ironically, religious groups and courts often use the same evidence to argue vastly different conclusions. Money and the "In God We Trust" motto is a case in point. While researching this story we discovered that the religious motto was often cited by religious groups as "proof" of the melding of government and faith, or in support of the notion that America is founded upon Christian religious principles. Other evidence included the opening of congressional sessions with prayer, the display of a Ten Commandments bas relief at the U.S. Supreme Court building, or the fact that the President of the United States takes the oath of office while swearing on a bible. The same sort of evidence, though, often appears in court rulings which decide establishment clause cases. Justices will

cite the "In God We Trust" motto, for example, as evidence of a "civic religion," or maintain that it has a secular intent.[16]

This obvious frustration with the normalization of the relation between the religionized identity of the currency and the nation is not lessened but only made more visible by the atheists' movement to deface the motto from the face of currency. This defacement of the currency seems to be the only option available for the secularists to remind the larger public of the irony of the religionized identity of the nation. But this option remains frustrating not simply because "defacement" is necessarily a negation of an object but, as anthropologist Michael Taussig puts it, "[defacement] also animates the thing defaced, and the mystery revealed may become more mysterious." If we follow Taussig's argument, we could argue that secularists remain frustrated because defacement does not adequately reveal the irony of the religious identity of the currency/nation since this identity now has become a "public secret," and by extension, has become the "truth."[17] Seen from this perspective, the public already knows the irony (and does not need being reminded of it) because knowing it is crucial to maintaining it as a public secret. Even though this way of understanding may be structurally useful, I wish to see it in a different (less structured) way. I see defacement as a frustrating labor for atheists because it involves the double task of questioning not only the religionized identity of the currency/nation, but also the law (Title 18 section 33) that prohibits any defacement of the currency. The questioning of one law is prohibited by another law. The atheists' frustration clearly borders on a profound sense of despair, almost tantamount to a total resignation to the law (indeed the "reality") of the religionized identity of the currency/nation. As the atheists write:

---

[16] 'In God We Trust'

[17] Michael Taussig, *Defacement: Public Secrecy and the Labor of the Negative* (Stanford: Stanford University Press, 1999), 2-6. On how publicity works as a secret and what is public is not necessarily helpful to democratic politics, see Jodi Dean, "Publicity's Secret," *Political Theory* 29 no. 5 (2001): 624-650.

One thing remains certain. Despite the convincing evidence that "In God We Trust" has a strong origin in religious sensibilities, it is doubtful that courts today would care to revisit O'HAIR v. BLUMENTHAL, or any other case which proposes to take up this controversial issue. Scratching out "In God We Trust," or stamping separationist slogans on the currency displays the frustration that many Atheists have in dealing with a legal system which rarely holds to a stern and strict interpretation of the establishment clause. The wall of separation goes only so far. You can bet your money on it.[18]

If we see this atheist/secularist despair as an implicit surrender to the post-first amendment law(s), to the "self-evidentness" of the religionized identity of an "originally" secular nation, then we must think of a strategy that can reach beyond law. To think beyond law, of course, is to think beyond history. As we have seen already, the secularists' insistence on the unconstitutionality of the In-God-We-Trust motto rests, to a large extent, on historicist claims, on returning to the history of the constitution/first amendment. This, of course, is their version of history, and some might challenge it. I am not interested in whether or not the atheists have gotten their history right. Rather my point here is that if what becomes possible at the end of the history they provide is merely this despair, then we must move beyond history.

But what is important to note is that this despair alone cannot make that move possible. It cannot do so because the demand of this despair—if one can call it that—is one that yearns for the restoration of the constitutional separation of church and religion. The demand of the despair remains anchored in history, in a history of the past. Thinking beyond this history, then, means giving up the commitment to what is being demanded in the despair, that is "history" itself. Giving up this commitment to history could be unthinkable for the secularists because it also involves recognizing the irrelevance of the very constitutional principle of the separation of church/state to the *contingent* demands of the present. After all, the laws that have made possible the imprinting

---

[18] "In God We trust"

of the motto on the currency were not accidental; they were historical products, products of debates in which specific individuals made particular claims for it, and the debates mark particular "changes"—if you will—in the history of the constitution. If one sees these laws as examples of how history changes, there is ample evidence to dismiss the secularists' desires to restore the "original" constitution. The secularists, then, will have to think of the unthinkable option of giving up their claims to history and construct arguments about history/time that will make available a different option: the option of the present. This option can be made available only through a theory of the present that disconnects itself from the past/history, a theory that seeks to understand the present's demands in relation to itself. But, as we will see later, it is also a theory that views the present as disconnected from itself. It is perhaps through such a renewed view of the present that the now seemingly impossible labor of repealing the so-called "unconstitutional" laws might begin to navigate toward the horizon of "unactualized possibility" (more on this below).

History after "But So What?"

As a way of contemplating this possibility, I want to turn to anthropologist David Scott's recent intervention in a postcolonial intellectual debate about Sri Lanka. My initial attempt at thinking about desecularizing secularism was indeed inspired by Scott's intervention to reshape the direction of the historicist debate about nationalism, the past, and identity in Sri Lanka. Since desecularizing secularism has a lot do with relinquishing certain kinds of secularist claims to history, thinking with and through Scott's call for dehistorizing history is both necessary and important. More importantly, meditating on the question of secularism in relation to the contemporary concerns of Sri Lanka, I think, can help us see how this ostensibly western debate about religion, history, and identity can find an unconventional ally in a postcolonial society. In this respect, the debate about the motto on US currency has far-reaching implications. This is not merely because the US currency (as one might quite rightly suggest) has become "globalized," disseminating the values of capitalism and secularism (though not necessarily democracy in some cases).[19] One might also argue that the US currency has no border-confined location or ownership, and thus, as secularists might contend, the "we" in the motto does epistemic violence by imposing a uniform religious identity on the global "secular" market.

I do not see the problem of secularism vis-à-vis the motto on the currency as a necessarily "global" matter. Rather, I view it as a debate bound up with a specific postcolonial concern because its key ideas (such as rights, citizenship, and nation-state) are part of the problematic of "modernity at large"—to use Appadurai's felicitous phrase—that animates the politics of postcolonial nationalism and post-secular belonging.[20] If we see the terms of the debate about the In-God-We-Trust in America as echoing the questions of a postcolonial debate in Sri Lanka, then reckoning with the former can be an intervention with postcolonial implications. If we think of the postcolonial intervention in a way in which we might intervene to suggest how different geo-political spaces with seemingly differing ethical concerns can converge to be unlikely allies in thinking about belonging in (post-secular) futures, then the usually taken-for-granted binaries of West/Other, minority/majority, Sinhalese/Tamil that have sustained modernity can begin to lose their moorings.[21] Locating the possibility of such

---

[19] Here, suffice it to say that the Bush administration's financial assistance to countries like Pakistan to help combat terrorism is precisely guided by the former's commitment to secularism, and not necessarily democracy. One has yet to conceptualize how this secularism might be different from that which failed in Iraq.

[20] In so many different ways, for sometime now, Dipesh Chakrabarty has been reminding us of the non-western partnership in the architecture of modernity. More than a decade ago Chakrabarty argued that "modernity is not the work of Europeans alone; the third-world nationalisms, as modernizing ideologies par excellence, have been equal partners in the process." See his seminal *Provincializing Europe: Post-Colonial Thought and Historical Difference* (Princeton: Princeton University Press, 2000), 43. The chapter on provincializing Europe first appeared in *Representations* in 1992.

[21] I use the word post-secular not to mean the end of the secular but to note something of the political present animated by the crisis of secularism, to which I allude in the paper. In this regard I disagree with Phillip Blond that rescuing religion from the hands of "fascists" as a corrective to the "liberal erasure of God" can be seen as "the end of the secular." See his introduction in Blond, ed., *The Post-Secular Philosophy: between Philosophy and Theology* (New York:

alliances can, at least, help us think beyond ever tightening (imagined or not) borders of citizenship in a so-called globalizing
world. This is how I wish to approach Scott's intervention in the
debate about history in Sri Lanka.

The debate Scott details is between two prominent scholars of ancient and medieval Sri Lankan history, R. A. L. H. Gunawardana and K. N. O. Dharmadasa. Trained in England and
Australia respectively, today both scholars hold academic positions at the prestigious Peradeniya University in Sri Lanka. The
debate between them is well-known among intellectuals in Sri
Lanka and Sri Lankanist scholars in the West. I think it safe to say
that while the works of the two historians are often cited in the
bibliographies of numerous academic works, on the whole the Sri
Lankanist scholars in the West remain deeply suspicious of if not
down right hostile to the politics of Dharmadasa's historiography.
Dharmadasa is viewed as a historian of a certain nationalist lean-
ing, defending, more or less explicitly, the ideological norms of the
Sinhala Buddhist chauvinism; Gunawardana is esteemed as a liberal historian with certain commitments to the politics of the left.
Now it is hard to deny that Gunawardana's liberal historiography
has an alluring political appeal to those of us writing about Sri
Lankan identity politics in the shadow of the island's two-decade
long separatist war. The debate between Gunawardana and
Dharmadasa, then, is not a narrow academic quarrel; it reflects
broader questions of nationalism, history, and minority belonging.
Despite Sri Lankanist scholars' familiarity with the debate, Scott's
intervention within it remains unknown at best and unappreci-
ated at worst, considering that it (entitled "Dehistoricising History") has appeared in two different venues since 1995.[22]
Obviously my concern is not so much with the nationalist debate

---

Routledge, 1998), 54. The possible dangers of "new traditionalist" criticisms of
secularism to democracy are the subject Jeff Stout's interesting *Democracy and
Tradition* (Princeton: Princeton University Press, 2004).

[22] It first appeared in Pradeep Jeganathan and Qadri Ismail, ed. *Unmaking the
Nation* (Colombo: Social Scientist Association, 1995), 10-24; and second in
Scott, *Refashioning Futures: Criticism after Postcoloniality* (Princeton: Princeton
University Press, 1999), 93-105. All references to the article are from *Refashion-
ing Futures*.

as it is with (a belated assessment of) the relevance of what Scott's intervention has to say to the problem of rethinking the relation between history and secularism in general. While I consider Scott's labor to dehistoricize history seminal, to be relevant to my task at hand, I will rethink it in terms of a post-Nietzschean idea of active forgetfulness of history.

"But so what?" This is the central question that Scott puts to the historicist debate in Sri Lanka. The question is first directed toward Gunawardana's lengthy historiographic essay "People of the Lion." This essay, which was first published in the 1970s, is, as Scott says, interested in showing not so much the political danger of Sinhala nationalism as the unsoundness of the nationalist history of Sri Lanka and the indefensibility of its political claims. Gunawardana's wager is that our contemporary understanding of the Sri Lankan past (history) has been saturated by Sinhala nationalist ideology, which among other things makes claims to the priority of the Sinhala race (as a numerical and a moral "majority") in Sri Lanka. This ideology has become normalized to such an extent that most Sri Lankan writers assume that it has "a very old history."(Note how eerily similar this is to what the atheists say about the history of the In-God-We-Trust motto. Gunawardana dismantles the edifice of this assumption piece-by-piece, carefully sifting through a massive pile of historical facts and myths, and demonstrates that the nationalist ideology has its history wrong. At least Gunawardana contends so. At the end of the "People of the Lion," Gunawardana, as Scott says, becomes a "historians' historian" wanting to relieve "us of our anxiety about the past of 'Sinhala.' Not only is the past rationally reconstructible within the ordered prose of professional history, but the evidence assembled pointedly demonstrates that history is, as it were, on our [liberal-progressivist] side" (101). The problem was that no sooner did Gunawardana—supported by other leftist intellectuals in Sri Lanka—rest assured of the soundness of his own reconstructed history than K.N.O Dharmadasa published his rebuttal, challenging the veracity of the former's findings. "Suddenly a fresh set of daunting questions seem to present themselves, questions about adequate data, sound scholarship, sources of evidence, strategies of reading, etc." (102). Loyal historian that he is, Gunawardana could think of no other critical strategy than crafting his own historicist rejoinder, full of new facts, to counter Dharmadasa's rebuttal.

This is the point of the debate at which Scott intervenes. In the wake of the rebuttal-after-rebuttal stalemate of this debate, Scott questions, "what if, at the end of...this masterful tour-de-force ["People of the Lion"], Gunawardana simply and deliberately asked: But so what? What does this history really prove? How does it help us decide the questions of political community in Sri Lanka today"(94)? Scott admits satirically that it will be difficult for a historian of Gunawardana's caliber to heed this ostensibly comical Nietzschean suggestion. "How could he, we would have asked ourselves incredulously, how could this esteemed professor of ancient and medieval Sri Lankan history, an historian so well known for his commitment to the craft, to the technologies of its muse, to its forms of narrative, to its orders of evidence, how could he in so singular and an intemperate a gesture, heed such thoughtless ridicule upon this distinguished practice of Truth?" (94). Simply put, Gunarwardana (perhaps as American atheists do) "believes too much in history." But had Gunawardana risked loyalty to his profession and asked the question "But so what?", "he would have disconnected the story of the past from the politics of the present and thus made itself invulnerable to historicist criticisms" (105). It would have delivered a severe blow to nationalists. Nationalists would no longer be able to argue with that question by resorting to history, and instead they would have to resort to the politics of the present in which that claim is located. To extend Scott's argument a bit, I would suggest that the strategy of making nationalists reckon with the politics of the present, in turn, would—as Foucault would have suggested—enable them to take more political risks, rendering unavailable the possibility of affirming the "innocence" of their history.

Scott's question of "But so what?" constitutes, for me, an unprecedented critical strategy to think about the problem of history vis-à-vis nationalism in Sri Lanka. But concerned as I am with the questions of secularism, history, and the In-God-We-Trust debate, I suspect that Scott's strategy requires more elaboration if it is to gain clarity as a political possibility. To be sure Scott grants that it is "not the penultimate gesture in…a getting *beyond*, so much as the initial move of what needs an extended elaboration." (105). What I am attempting here is a step forward such an extended elaboration. Needless to say my attempt is by no means exhaustive. My modest proposition is that the question of "But so what?" may be viewed as a post-Nietzschean political possibility if we think of it in relation to Nietzsche's idea of "active forgetfulness" coupled with Derrida's meditation on Hamlet's overture "time is out of joint." If it aims at disconnecting the history of the past from the politics of the present, forgoing the past's relevance to the politics of the present, Scott's question needs to be rethought in relation to a possibility of forgetting. My wager here is that to think of such a possibility of forgetting, we need a conceptualization of not only the present as a moment of disjuncture, a moment in which time is out of joint, disjointed and disconnected from the past/history; we also need to think how that moment of disjuncture might become "the very possibility of the other" (*Specters of Marx*, 22). This possibility of the other can become justice, that is, justice without history/law.

Active Forgetfulness and the Ghostly Present:
Nietzsche and Derrida

The practice of forgetting, as I conceive it, is not a passive form or static being. It does the "active" work of ceasing to re-member/re-member the past vis-à-vis the present. This notion of active forgetting hearkens back to Nietzsche. Nietzsche introduces it in his classic essay "On the Uses and Disadvantages of History for Life." Here Nietzsche speaks of the "art and the power of forgetting" as a way of "delivery from the malady of history."[23] This is possible through the practice of the unhistorical. For Nietzsche, the art of forgetting and the "unhistorical" are interrelated. As he says, the "the ability to forget, or to put it in a more scholarly fashion, the capacity to feel *unhistorically* during its duration" is

---

[23] Nietzsche. Untimely Meditations, ed. R. J. Hollingdale (Cambridge: Cambridge University Press, 1983), 122.

more or less the same. Concerned as he is with "history for the purposes of life," that is to say, history for the future, Nietzsche insists that "the historical sense no longer conserves life but mummifies it"(75). He detests what he calls the "the historical sense without restraint." "When the historical sense...*without restraint* reigns supreme, and all its consequences are realized, it uproots the future"(95). On this view, to be unhistorical is by extension to be concerned with the future.

Nietzsche does not want to abandon the historical altogether. He wants to have a balance between the historical and the unhistorical. This balance, by extension, is a balance between remembering and forgetting ("to forget at the right time so as to remember at the right time" [63]). This balance is *necessary in equal measure for the health of an individual, of a people and of a culture*"(63). The lack of this balance results in the historical sense reigning supreme and taking over life and its future. "With an excess of history man ceases...to exist" (64). On this account, forgetting is a way of restoring life and the act of living to the present. "Forgetting is essential to any kind of action." This act of living life in forgetting is one located in the present. For Nietzsche, in this present of forgetting, "every moment really dies, sinks back into night and fog, and is extinguished for ever" (61). Now, my point is that this present, it seems to me, must have a particular relation to the future. If Nietzsche, as quoted above, contends that "history uproots the future," the present he speaks of must be related to the future. But Nietzsche's understanding of the future is very different from that of the "historical men." This difference is captured when he says,

> looking to the past impels...[historical men] towards the future and fire[s] their courage to go on living and their hope that what they want will still happen, that happiness lies behind the hill they are advancing towards. These historical men believe that the meaning of existence will come more and more to light in the course of its *process*, and they glance behind them only so that, from the process so far, they can learn to understand the present and desire the future more vehemently (65).

Seen in this anti-Hegelian way, the future is hardly the culmination of a "process." One cannot desire to arrive at the future by merely passing through the present. Better yet, one cannot hope to bypass the present, hoping for a better future. One cannot wait for the end of the present at which point one leaps on to the future. The future is not just beyond the present, not just beyond the hill, that one marches towards. One cannot inhabit the present and anticipate reaching the future this way. *It cannot be anticipated this way because the present is not only disconnected from the past or the future but also disconnected from itself.* It is disconnected from itself because in it "every moment really dies, sinks back into night and fog, extinguished for ever" (61). One cannot escape this ever dying, ever extinguishing moment of the present as one who is drowning in a swirling eddy of water may struggle to reach the surface for a gasp of air and eventually reach the shore of safety. To be in this Nietzschean present is to be fully caught up in its dying moment. In other words, if there is any future, one has to find that future in the present. Such a future, as Heidegger would have suggested, is not that which will be. The future is the present that already is (extinguishing).[24]

Now my point here is that if the task of forgetting is possible at all, it is possible only in the present because one cannot practice forgetting for the sake of the future. At the same time, if forgetting is possible in the ever-extinguishing moment of the present, it must be so for the sake of the present. As we will see below, this forgetting is possible in the present precisely because the present is marked by its vanishing moments or the moments of it constantly being disconnected, disjointed from itself. But there is another point to be made about forgetting and its relation to living in the dying moment of the present. Nietzsche's idea of living with(in) forgetting is not at all akin to "living without memory." Forgetting is not a form of amnesia or inertia. Nietzsche grants that people may live without memory and even be happy. Yet he asserts that "it is altogether impossible to *live* at all without forgetting" (62). Note that what Nietzsche is doing is carefully sepa-

---

[24] For an interesting take on the idea of the future in relation to Heidegger's "not yet," see Chakrabarty, Provincializing Europe, 249-253.

rating the practice of living with(in) forgetting from that of living without memory. This is clear when he contrasts forgetting to sleepiness of the historical. Sleepiness of the historical, he stresses, is dangerous. *"There is a degree of sleepiness...of the historical which is harmful and even fatal to the living thing, whether this living thing be a man, or a people, or a culture"* (ibid.). Forgetting then is hardly sleepiness. It is an active practice. Nietzsche elaborates on the active sense of forgetting in the *Genealogy of Morals* albeit with a certain psychological gloss on it.

> Forgetfulness is no mere vis inertiae as the superficial imagine; it is rather an active and in the strictest sense positive faculty of repression, that is responsible for the fact that what we experience and absorb enters our consciousness as little while we are digesting it (one might call the process "inpsychation") as does the thousand fold process, involved in physical nourishment--so-called 'incorporation.' To close the doors and windows of consciousness for a time; to remain undisturbed by the noise and struggle of our underworld of utility organs, working with and against one another; a little quietness, a little tabula rasa of the consciousness, to make room for new things, above all for the nobler functions and functionaries, for regulations, foresight, premeditation (for our organism is an oligarchy)--that is the purpose of active forgetfulness, which is like a doorkeeper, a preserver of psychic order, repose, and etiquette; so that it will be immediately obvious how there could be no happiness, no cheerfulness, no hope, no pride, no present, without forgetfulness.[25]

If there can be no happiness, no living, no present, without this forgetfulness, then forgetting and the present are not two separate strategies of being. Just as forgetting becomes possible in the present, so the present becomes possible in forgetting. They constantly animate each other. The possibility of this mutual relation between forgetting and the present, between forgetting and

---

[25] Cited in James Soderholm, "Byron, Nietzsche, and the Mystery of Forgetting," *CLIO*, 23(1)(1993): 51-63. Soderholm is primarily concerned with Nietzsche's interest in Lord Byron's hero Manfred.

living, can be grasped better if we view it in light of Derrida's recent effort to think of the question of justice vis-à-vis the (Hamletian) overture of "time-is-out-of-joint." This is crucial because forgetting, as I think with Nietzsche, is a strategy of coming to terms with the "disjointedness" of the present. The disjointedness of the present is precisely where Derrida contends that the question of justice remains to be asked. Hence, if forgetting for Nietzsche is about happiness, about living, and about the present, then for Derrida forgetting (as a synonym for the disjointedness of time) is about the possibility of justice. Put simply, Nietzsche's contention that there can be no happiness without forgetting is fundamentally about justice, and we need to pass through Derrida to grasp better the relation between forgetting, justice, and the present.

Derrida's meditation on Hamlet's gesture of time-is-out-joint is positioned against Fukuyama's neo-evangelist announcement of the "end of history." This announcement was generated by, among other things, the supposed collapse of Marxism as a political possibility, an announcement masqueraded as an "event." Derrida's meditation is pervaded by a particular interest in the figure of the specter or the ghost. For Derrida to meditate on the figure of the ghost is to meditate on the disjointedness of time. He thinks about the relation between the figure of the ghost and the disjointedness of history vis-à-vis the celebrated death of Marxism. If Marxism is dead, one can only speak of its "non-presence" (101). For Derrida, the figure of the ghost is synonymous with this non-presence. This means that if we are to talk about Marxism, we can only talk about its specters, ghosts, and apparitions. (Derrida begins with Marx's opening line in the *Communist Manifesto* that "a specter is haunting Europe." Marx, of course, does not like ghosts because he prefers the material, the real, too much.) Just as specters can never assume a content of being, Marxism can perhaps never really materialize. But Marx's ghosts haunt us.[26] "The ghost never dies, it always remains to come, and

---

[26] Now, it is important to point out that Derrida considers himself hardly a Marxist. But he is against the European alliances (as he calls them) to exorcise and chase away the ghost of Marx, too quickly. As he puts it, literally and meta-

to come back" (99). But the "specter will never be there. There is no *Dasein* [being] of the specter." Yet the specter does have a "certain visibility." It is "the visibility of the invisible." "And visibility, by its essence, is not seen, which is why it remains…beyond the phenomenon, or beyond being."(100)

There is a particular relation between the ghost and the present. When Derrida says that the ghost "remains to come," he is not speaking of an "event" that will happen in the future. Far from it. There is no relation between the specter and the future (as that which will be) because the specter has no being that it can take into the future. The specter's invisible presence, the "visibility of the invisibility," is fleeting; it comes and goes, appears and disappears. It cannot be anticipated nor apprehended. This "place of spectrality" is synonymous with the present that is out of joint with itself. It is the place where one may await "what one does not expect yet or any longer" (65). This is Derrida's ghostly history. Inhabited by specters appearing and disappearing, flitting in and out of sight, the ghostly present is where one cannot await what one wants. One can not await what one expects in this present because the present does not march or progress forward. As Wendy Brown puts it: "In Derrida's reformulation, history emerges as that which shadows and constrains, incites and thwarts, rather than that which directs and unfolds. History as a ghostly phenomenon does not march forward, rather it comes and goes, appears and recedes, materializes and evaporates… It changes shape."[27]

If the present is the place of spectrality, the ghostly present, the fleeting present, it is in such a present that one must do the almost impossible work of "thinking justice," justice without an "event," without history, without right, and without law (65). Justice seems almost impossible without history (to most of

---

phorically, Marx "belongs to a time of disjunction, to that 'time out of joint' in which is inaugurated, laboriously, painfully, tragically, a new thinking of borders, a new experience of the house, the home, and the economy. He is not part of the family, but one should not send him back, once again, him too, to the border (174).

[27] Wendy Brown, *Politics out of History* (Princeton: Princeton University Press, 2001), 151.

us), and Derrida is proposing the seemingly impossible because the present where justice is to be thought is deprived of any recourse to history. What makes (thinking) justice possible in the present is the present's own disjointure, and that present cannot have recourse to history. "The necessary disjointure, the detotalizing condition of justice, is indeed here that of the present—and by the same token the very condition of the present, and of the very presence of the present" (28). If this present has any contemporaneity in this disjointed present, that contemporaneity is ghostly. And this is why he speaks of what he calls "the non-contemporaneity with itself of the living present" (xix). This is the disjointed present; this is the time out of joint.

Derrida does not see any hope in understanding justice in the disjointure of the present in terms of the familiar vocabularies of *doing* or *rendering* justice. Such a conception of justice smacks too much of a politics of "restitution," a politics in which one merely gives justice to the "other" (27). "Thinking justice," as he calls it, should move beyond this juridical, restitutional, reparational politics of justice. Restitutional justice always needs history, right, and law. Justice by means of restitutional politics becomes justice by means of "punishment, payment, expiation." This is what he calls justice with "vengeance." Such justice operates within the horizon of culpability, debt, right, and accountability (25), and Derrida wants to rescue justice from such juridical connotations. Indeed, when Derrida says that "law and right stem from vengeance," one can think of many instances of how justice is usually sought within juridical and non-juridical domains—from national courtrooms to international organizations like the South African Truth and Reconciliation Committee.[28] Even non-juridical, non-state organizations are concerned with law and right, and this is precisely the case with the American Atheists' Organization. All these juridically minded organizations undoubtedly do some sort of "justice." But Derrida's contention here is that justice conceived in terms of law or right is

---

[28] For Derrida's take on the South African Truth and Reconciliation Committee, see his "On Forgiveness" in *On Cosmopolitanism and Forgiveness: Thinking in Action*, eds. Simon Critchley and Richard Kearney (New York: Routledge, 2001).

often a way of doing or giving justice to the other as the *other*. This is why Derrida asks: "if right or law stems from vengeance, as Hamlet seems to complain that it does—before Nietzsche, before Heidegger, before Benjamin—can one not yearn for justice that one day, a day belonging no longer to history, a quasi-messianic day, would finally be removed from the fatality of vengeance?" (21).

What I want to underscore is that Derrida's attempt at thinking justice beyond accountability, law, right, etc. in the disjointure of the present that no longer belongs to history establishes a particular political-ethical relation to the other, a new way of conceiving the other, an other "not yet *there*." To do this, Derrida suggests that we give up thinking of justice in terms of giving or doing justice to the other. Thinking beyond this sort of distributive justice is an important way to divest justice of any association with law or right or accountability. One might, of course, ask: Can one think of justice as a gift so as to separate it from any link to law or right, a gift that belongs not to the giver, not even to God, but only to the other? Derrida would respond with a counter question: even if one were to understand justice as a gift beyond accountability, calculation, and commerce, "the gift to the other as gift of that which one does not have, and which thus, paradoxically, can only come back and belong to the other, is there not a risk of inscribing this whole moment of justice under the sign of presence?" (27). Put alternatively, the idea of justice as a gift, whether it is beyond law or commerce, or whether it ultimately comes back and belongs to the other, presupposes the existence of justice somewhere in the present, under "the sign of presence," pointing to it being *there*. This way of thinking about justice presupposes not only that justice exists out *there*; but that the other, as the other (or as the victim), also always exists out *there*, waiting to receive justice. Clearly, for Derrida neither justice nor the other needing justice exists under a sign of presence. One cannot merely see them *there*. They are neither apprehensible nor identifiable. They do not wait under the sign of presence. They cannot because they have no apprehensible *dasein*. They cannot because the sign of presence cannot exist in the disjunctured present. If "disjuncture is the very possibility of the other," and if the disjunctured present is the ghostly present, neither justice nor the other can possibly remain out *there*. So we may ask: how might we speak of justice and the other if we cannot find and apprehend them under a sign of presence? Derrida's answer would be: "not yet *there*." For Derrida to speak of justice "not yet *there*" is simultaneously to speak of the other as not yet *there* as well. Thus, by extension, the question of justice becomes a question of the other.

> Of justice where it is not yet, not yet *there*, where it is no longer, let us understand where it is no longer *present*, and where it will never be, no more than the law, reducible to laws or rights... No justice—let us not say no law and once again we are not speaking here of laws—seems possible or thinkable without some *responsibility*, beyond all living present, within that which disjoins the living present, before the ghosts of those who are not yet born, or those who are already dead, be they victims of wars, political or other kinds of violence, nationalist, racist, colonialist, sexist, or other kinds of exterminations, victims of capitalists imperialisms, or any of the forms of totalitaranisms. *Without this non-contemporaneity with itself of the living present*, without that which secretly unhinges it, without this responsibility, and without this respect for justice, concerning those who *are not there*, of those who are no longer yet *present and living*, what sense would there be to ask the question "where?," "where tomorrow?, "whither?"

What is important to note here is that the phrases "not yet there," "not yet born," "no longer present," and "will never be" do not simply mean that justice and the ghostly others have no location. Rather they are strategic terms to speak of the *ghostly location*, if you will, of justice and the other, the place of spectrality. If they exist, that is, if they are possible at all, they are possible only in the ghostly present. If the ghostly, disjunctured present is the very possibility of the other, it is also the possibility of justice and vice versa.

For Derrida, to think of the possibility of justice and the other within this ghostly present is to think of their possibility "beyond all living present." Just as those others who are not yet born, or those others who are victims of wars and violence of all types, those who are already dead or who are presently living, the question of justice and the other can concern all of us, the dead, the living, and the yet to be born. The question of justice must "carry beyond the *present* life" (xx). But justice beyond *present* life does not merely appeal to a better future. For Derrida, the appeal to such a future is neither acceptable nor possible. One cannot appeal to such a future because one cannot leave behind the already dead and the presently living; one cannot appeal to such a future because one cannot just leap onto the future from the disjointed present. This is why he disagrees with neo-evangelist futurists who fantasize "there is even a more final end of history to come," supposedly after the complete universalization of democracy and capitalism. Such futurists consider a future "necessary" for the supposed well being of the world. This necessity—expressed in terms of we "must/should" aspire to a better future—becomes just another "law." ("'...it is necessary' is necessary, and *that is the law*" [73].) All this law does is that it dislodges the present out of its "contemporaneity with itself" (73). But inhabiting as we do the ghostly present, the disjointed present, we cannot appeal to such a future. The disjointed present has no contemporaneity with itself. It does not because time is out of joint. This is why Derrida speaks the "non-contemporaneity with itself of the living present." If any justice, if any future, is to be located, it has to be located in the non-contemporaneity with itself of the living present.

Only by inhabiting—I admit this is a bad word—the non-contemporaneity with itself of the living present, can one think of the question of justice as a possibility beyond the living present. As he says, "if it is possible, and if one takes it seriously, the possibility of the question of justice, which is perhaps no longer a question, and which we are calling here *justice*, must carry beyond *present* life, life as *my* life, or *our* life. *In general*. For it will be the same thing for the "my life" or "our life" tomorrow, that is for the life of others, as it was yesterday for the other others." *Beyond therefore the living present in general* (xx). Note the importance of what Derrida is saying here. The non-contemporaneity with itself of the living present then makes it impossible to think justice within one temporal domain or in relation to one ethnic or reli-

gious community that we might call mine or ours. Indeed, conceiving justice this way makes it possible to transcend—so to
speak—ethnically or religiously bounded notions of us and them,
citizen and alien. This is precisely because it has no contemporaneity with itself; it is off hinges. Inhabiting this ghostly present,
one cannot leave behind the past or its atrocities or injustices for
the sake of a utopian future that will happen one day; nor can
one simply remain attached to a supposedly stable past and resist
the future-to-come. The past and the future have only the relevance they do in the ghostly present. The past and the future are
ghosts. Ghosts do not belong to, remain attached to time, that is,
to specific temporal location (xx). If Derrida speaks (as he does)
of ghosts of the dead and ghosts of the yet to be born, he must
mean that past and the future can belong nowhere else but in the
ghostly present. In this ghostly present, they appear and disap-
pear; they haunt us, all of us. They cannot be conjured, exorcised,
and sent back to the proper place of their "presence." They must
be engaged seriously and responsibly. This is why perhaps Derrida
characterizes the time of the ghostly present as "not a time whose
joinings are negated, broken, mistreated, dysfunctional, disad-
justed, according to a *dis*-of negative opposition and dialectical
disjunction, but a time without *certain* joining, a determinable
conjunction" (18). Clearly, Derrida does not want to disregard
and negate the past and whatever its (famous or infamous) en-
tailments, imagined or not, merely because they are the past. If
one were to take the past seriously, one can do so only in the disconnected present. It is in the disjointed present that the past's
possible joining or relevance to the present (or the future) can be
constructed. This is what I think Derrida means when he says:
"To maintain together that which does not hold together, and the
disparate itself, ...all of this can be thought...only in a dislocated
time of the present, at the joining of a radically dis-jointed time,
without a certain conjunction"(17).

The critical point I want to make here is this: in so-far-as
the disconnected present is where one has to labor to "maintain
together that which does not hold together," the possibility of forgoing (forgetting) that which does not hold together can become
available. In other words, we need Derrida's ghostly present to

make better sense of Nietzsche's active forgetting. Nietzsche's idea of how forgetting becomes possible in the present, and the present in forgetting, gains greater clarity when we see it in tandem with Derrida's conceptualization of the spectral present that is disjointed with itself. If Nietzsche's present is where every moment dies, sinks back into night and fog, extinguishing forever and Derrida's notion of the ghostly present is haunted by the untraceable and unmappable appearance and disappearance of ghostly moments, then forgetting in such a present can become a ghostly reality, if you will. That is, granted that the ghostly present is haunted by disjointed traces, traces that can be conjoined only by a disciplinary tool such as history or anthropology, forgetting such traces of history (a history of what happened prior to us in the past, or who did what to us), becomes synonymous with the ghostly present. That is, if one wants to "live on" (Derrida's words) in this ghostly present one must forget. So forgetting is about living. But how can this forgetting in the ghostly present produce justice (for Derrida) and happiness (for Nietzsche)? To understand this we need to meditate on how forgetting as a ghostly reality might become a kind of political possibility.

Justice can only be a possibility because it is "not yet *there*"; if it is not yet *there* one can only think justice. In the way I conceive them, thinking bears a particular relation to possibility. As Theodor Adorno once said, "thinking is not the intellectual reproduction of what already exists any way....thinking has a secure hold on possibility."[29] On the other hand, following Heidegger, as Chakrabarty has reminded us, a possibility should be thought of as "the unrealized actual." "For a possibility to be neither that which is waiting to become actual nor that which is merely incomplete, the possible has to be thought as that which already actually *is* but is present only as the 'not yet' actual" (*Provincializing Europe*, 249-250). It is in these senses that I conceive of forgetting as an unactualized political possibility, a possibility of justice. In other words, the possibility of forgetting is the

---

[29] Theodor Adorno, "Resignations," in *Critical Model: Interventions and Catchwords* (New York: Columbia University Press, 1998), 292.

possibility of justice; the possibility of justice is, in turn, the possibility of the other. One cannot think justice without thinking (about and with) the other. To get at the relations among the trio of forgetting, justice, and other, I turn, once again, to Sri Lanka. I want to think briefly about forgetting in relation to two vastly disjointed "incidents" in 1983 and 2001. (For the sake of clarity here, I use the word incidents. I think, as it will be evident soon, it is better to call them "dates.") To stress the obvious, such incidents do not at all constitute for me empirical examples of how forgetting ought to be done. Rather, the way I read these two incidents to conceptualize an immeasurable disjointure between them and thereby contemplate the possibility of active forgetting will be very different from an empirical account of "why" they happened.

The Possibility of "Non-Presence" without Explanation

July 23, 1983, Sri Lanka. The date is synonymous with the riots that put Sri Lanka on the global map as a dangerous zone of pulverizing "ethnic" violence and political instability. The riots undoubtedly created a black hole, interrupting post-colonial Sri Lanka's self-proclaimed capitalist march toward its political modernity and mutli-culturalism, inaugurated by the postcolonial politics of the Jayewardene state that at once privileged a romantic version of Buddhism and de-privileged the role of Buddhist monks in politics.[30] Coordinated and anticipated, the July riots are often thought to have "erupted" in the wake of the ambush and decapitation of some thirteen members of the Sri Lankan armed forces by the LTTE (Liberation Tigers of Tamil Elam) that would later wage, for almost two decades, a devastating guerilla campaign for a separate state in northern Sri Lanka. During the riots, which lasted for a few days, arguably with tacit approval from government officials, gangs of armed Sinhalese men systematically and brutally killed more than three thousand innocent

---

[30] I have spelled out these details in my *Colors of the Robe: Religion, Identity, and Difference* (Columbia: University of South Carolina Press, 2004).

Tamil civilians, and looted and destroyed their properties and businesses worth billions, eventually displacing about one hundred thousand others throughout the country. Literature on the pogrom remains vast and has gained almost canonical status. I need not rehearse the arguments of that literature here except to note that they offer varying explanations with pronounced emphasis on the "causes" of the riots. Such causal explanations boil down to equations such as: LTTE ambush=>July riots, or Sinhala Buddhist hegemony=>LTTE ambush=>July riots.[31] Now I want to say that such causal explanations are neither impossible nor unhelpful ways of making sense of what happened. But I am not interested in such causal explanations here because I do not want necessarily to make sense of the riots in terms of the task at hand here. I do not want to make sense of the riots because doing so would make it easy for me to make sense of the next incident/date to which I will allude soon. In other words, explaining the July riots by way of the above equations will make readily available an explanation of an incident later and disjointed from the former. I am not interested in explaining this second incident because I am interested in thinking of a possibility. Explanation cannot make possibility available; explanation kills possibility. Explanation kills the ghostly present where possibility is thinkable. In the universe of explanation, there cannot be ghosts; they all remain fully exposed, apprehended, located, and mapped. The traces of the ghosts--where they have come from and where they will go--are all known and knowable in the universe of explanation.

The second incident I have selected also occurs in the month of July, but it is separated by a temporal gap of almost eighteen years from the July riots of 1983. On July 23, 2001, around three o'clock in the morning, a suicide squad of the LTTE penetrated and attacked Sri Lanka's tightly guarded international airport at Katunayaka. There were only a few casualties; five Sri Lankan soldiers and thirteen Tamil rebels were killed in the exchange of gunfire. But the attack caused colossal damage to Sri

---

[31] Pradeep Jeganathan's work has cast doubt on these sorts of explanations of violence. See *After a Riot: Anthropological Locations of Violence* (Ph.D Disst., University of Chicago, 1997).

Lanka's already crippled economy and military. Using shoulder-fired missiles, the rebels destroyed eight military aircraft and five commercial airplanes parked on the tarmac. The airport shut down for fourteen hours. International flights to Sri Lanka diverted to other countries, and subsequently major western airlines refused to resume flights to the island. The attack on the airport sharpened the internationalized images of Sri Lanka as a war zone. Commentaries by local and international political pundits offer varying explanations of "why" the attack took place: the attack was yet another indication of the seriousness of the LTTE's persistent demand for a separate state in the Northeast;[32] it was a retaliation against the Sri Lankan military, which refused to suspend its aerial bombings on rebel positions, despite a unilaterally declared LTTE cease-fire and a request for peace talks almost eight months prior to the attack; or it was merely another effort to further weaken the island's largely spent military force, and so on.

These explanations may all be on the mark. What is noteworthy is that however differently cast their explanations were, many of the commentaries on the attack included a distinct reference to the incident/date of the July riots of 1983. At first sight this reference seemed inevitable since the date of the airport attack corresponded to that of the July riots. But this reference was not just a reference to the corresponding dates between the two incidents. For some commentators to write about the airport attack was to not only to allude to the brutality of the July riots but also to recall briefly the entire history of the conflict between the LTTE and the Sri Lankan state, albeit with a certain sense of supposed objectivity. It seems that an LTTE attack of any proportion today can hardly be reported without some reference to the "leading" event of the 1983 July riots. (This is like the US secularists finding it difficult to speak of any contemporary issue concerning religion and public sphere without mentioning the First Amendment.) It is as if there must always be some connection between

---

[32] I have in mind an assortment of articles one can easily find on the web by typing the words "LTTE attack on the Katunayaka Airport in Sri Lanka" into a search engine like Google.

the past and the present, the old and the new, the leading and the following, the preceding and the subsequent. The question I want to ask regarding the two incidents/dates is this: why is establishing a connection between them critical? Is it because the connection seems self-evident? Can one write about a potential present/future LTTE attack with no reference to the supposedly leading event of 1983 so that a present/future attack may be seen in relation to its own domain of occurrence? Can one, in other words, forget the leading and the original? If so, at which point may one forget it?

It seems that the journalistic desire to establish a connection between July 23, 1983 and July 23, 2001 was premature at best, and untenable at worst, since the airport attack and its aftermath lacked a major feature that to-date defines the leading event of July 1983. There were no riots on or after July 23, 2001! There were no marauding mobs of Sinhalese men rampaging through the streets and looting Tamil businesses and killing Tamil civilians, either in the vicinity of the airport attack or elsewhere in Sri Lanka. (Indeed there had been no such Sinhala riots—certainly not of the egregious ilk of the 1983 July riots—notwithstanding numerous LTTE suicidal attacks on Sinhalese civilians and state targets.) If there were no riots on July 23, 2001, what other constituent features make the connection between the two dates conceivable? Is it the name LTTE? That is to say, the LTTE that ambushed and killed the thirteen soldiers, triggering the riots of 1983, is the same as the LTTE that attacked the Katunayaka airport. If this connection between the airport attack and July riots is based on the self-evident identity of the LTTE, it is more than a connection between two dates. That connection represents a particular distinction between two people: Sinhalese and Tamils. After all, the LTTE is claiming to be fighting for a separate state for Tamils. I think it safe to say that today it is all but impossible for political commentators to talk about the LTTE and the Tamils without talking about the Sinhalese. So my point here is that to draw a connection between July 23, 2001 and July 23, 1983 is to point to the difference between the Sinhalese and the Tamils. Seen in this way, an attack on the state (the airport and the military base) becomes (for the journalists and perhaps for the LTTE as well) an extension of the conflict between the Sinhalese majority and Tamil minority. At the end of establishing this connection between the two dates, between the leading and the following, explaining the following with a reference to the leading, the Sinhalese and the Tamils come to stand as they did in 1983 if not prior to that year. They remain the same; nothing has changed; there are no altered views of the relations between them; no altered ethos towards the separatist war on the part of the Sinhalese or the Tamils who might have no direct stakes in the politics of the Sri Lankan state or the LTTE. The LTTE just continue to attack its designated targets and the government continues to retaliate and vice versa.

My wager here is that the supposed connection between the two dates/incidents can be sustained only by explaining them, accounting for "why" they happened. To explain one incident is to explain the other; to explain the two incidents is to establish a connection between them. But explaining these two dates and establishing a connection between them, as must be evident so far, is to leave one striking aspect unexplained and unaccounted for: the absence or "non-presence" of riots on July 23, 2001. This absence or non-presence has to be left unexplained because it inevitably threatens to disconnect July 23, 2001 from July 23, 1983. The unavoidable question that one must pose here is this: can this absence be explained? My answer is that it can be done, but only at the risk of explanation itself, that is, if we understand explanation as a task of establishing connections between disjointed dates in this case. But explaining this absence will not be easy. If explanation of an event is about establishing connections, then it is about accounting for what has already happened, connecting the dots between the reality of one incident and the reality of another. They can be explained because they have happened; they are actualities; they belong to history; they have agents, subjects, and names, and dates (LTTE, Tamils, Sinhalese, July 1983, July 2001, and so on). But can one explain that which has not happened, that which is non-presence, that which is absence? Put differently, can one establish a connection between that which has happened and that which has not happened, between the presence of riots in 1983 and the non-presence of riots in 2001? I suppose one can.

But to do that one will have to privilege the leading event. In other words, one cannot ask why no riots took place on July 23, 2001 without asking why the riots took place on July 23, 1983. So long as one asks the question why no riots took place on July 23, 2001, one cannot ever disconnect it from July 23, 1983. So long as one asks the question of "why" (or "why not") one always remembers the leading event or the date. This is why, perhaps, Nietzsche once remarked that the question of "why" [or why not"] always presupposes a master subject. Slightly amending this, I would say that the question "why" always presupposes a leading, master, original event.

Now, of course, the journalists never bothered to notice the absence of riots on July 23, 2001, let alone ask the question "why" not. Had they even noticed this absence, it is clear, they would not have been able to account for it, at least not that easily. What I want to point out is not the journalistic inability to account for this absence. Indeed, what I want to suggest is that we forgo precisely this question of "why" the riots never happened if we are to think about this non-absence of riots as a particular kind of possibility. In other words, what I am suggesting is that if one is to disconnect the leading event from the following, one will have to notice this absence. But one will have to refuse the temptation of asking the question of why not. The moment we refuse this "why not," we refuse the temptation of explanation. The moment we are bereft of the temptation of explanation, we may have a different option of thinking about this seemingly hollow moment marked by the absence or non-presence.

My gamble is that the absence of riots on July 23, 2001 can be constituted as the space in which a certain kind of forgetting was possible. The absence of riots constitutes, for me, something of the Nietzschean dying moment or the Derridian ghostly present that is out of joint with itself; it is the moment that remains disconnected from the leading event of 1983. This hollow, empty moment of absence cannot be grasped or apprehended in relation to a moment or an event. It has no visible traces pointing to a location where it came from. It has no identifiable subject that engineered it. The absence is not necessarily a *result* of anything; it is not *conditioned by* anything; it did not even emerge; it was just absence; it was non-presence. If we need a name for this empty moment of absence/non-presence, we may call it the moment of forgetting. If absence/non-presence was conditioned by anything, it was conditioned only by forgetting. But forgetting has no actor(s) or agent(s) behind it—not in the way I seek to think about it. There is no group of people—call them Sinhalese—who are responsible for forgetting. Nobody did it. In other words, riots did not happen because the Sinhalese people had just forgotten, actively or not, their past sour relations with the imagined Tamil others and hence did not riot. Even if this is "why" no riots took place—a fact I suspect could not be easily verified by empirical data—I refuse to think so because it runs the risk of equating forgetting with an action. Forgetting is not an action that belongs to a people. I do not want to think of it as something that the Sinhalese did for themselves or for the Tamils or even for peace. If forgetting is such an action of doing by a people, it can never be "justice;" it can only be distributive justice.

Now what I want to emphasize here is that the moment of this forgetting, this moment of the non-presence of riots—has a certain active sense. For me it is active in the sense that we—the Tamils and the Sinhalese—cannot forget or allow ourselves to forget the carnage of the July riots of 1983. But that carnage cannot be the condition of the absence of the riots on Jul 23, 2001. It cannot be the condition of the absence because the possibility of the absence is located in the disjunctured, ghostly present that is out of joint and non-contemporaneous with itself. What is crucial to note is that though it is located in the disjointed present, we cannot talk about the absence of riots without some sense of the presence of riots somewhere—call this somewhere July 1983. This is logically impossible: one cannot talk about non-presence without some sense of presence; one cannot talk about death without some sense of life. Simply put, for something to be absent, non-present, something other must be or had to be present. Hence the non-presence of riots/active forgetfulness is not a total obliteration or denying of the presence of the July riots of 1983. The July riots of 1983 may be remembered; we may think of those who killed and those who died; but they have no bearing on the disjunctured present marked by the absence of riots. They cannot determine the outcome of July 23, 2001 because the very "outcome"—if you call the absence an outcome—immediately disconnects it from the riots of 1983. The importance of seeing this absence as made possible by the disjunctured moment of active forgetting—without a master engineer—is that it can become the space in which Tamils and Sinhalese might belong and become anew, form new relations, and "live on." This space of the absence, of course, is rapidly dying; perhaps it is already dead. If this space is already dead, the Tamils and Sinhalese already met each other there. They met each other without vengeance, without demands for apologies or forgiveness for what one people did to the other in the past. They could not demand and accuse each other because they met without the aid of history, law, or state; they met without a third party intervening to negotiate political settlements. They met in an active forgetting of history; they met in the absence, in the non-presence, of riots. They met in the moment of disconnection, in the non-contemporaneity with itself of the living present. This moment of meeting without history, law, and state is, perhaps, the moment of "justice," justice for those who are already dead, those who are living, and those who are yet to be born. But it is no transcendental justice. It does not cut across generations. Rather, the possibility of that justice is the possibility of the hollow moment in which we must "live on." Such justice, in the words of Wendy Brown, remains "detached from futurity, or confined to a self-identical present. But not only must justice have futurity—it is what *makes* futurity, in so far as it generates the future's relationship to the present as a 'living on' of present efforts and aims. Justice entails the present generation's responsibility for crafting continuity, as well as the limits of that responsibility and that continuity."[33]

The next time an LTTE attack or a state offensive against the LTTE or a riot takes place, those Tamils and Sinhalese who met in active forgetfulness in the hollow moment of the absence of riots on July 23, 2001, will have no relation to them; they will stand disconnected and disjointed from them. Data-mongering

---

[33] Brown, *History out of Politics*, 147.

journalists, anthropologists, and political pundits who will continue to write about Sri Lankan history and politics can neither afford to forget the dead, ghostly present of July 23 2001; nor can they link it to possible future attacks, counterattacks, and riots; nor can they include it on a list tracing the "history" of the conflict between the Sri Lankan state and the LTTE, returning to the leading event of the July riots of 1983.[34] That moment of the absence is dead. The ghosts of the Sinhalese and the Tamils who met in that absence will haunt any attempt either at facilely linking July 23, 2001 to July 23, 1983 or at conveniently forgetting them for the sake of the future.

To sum up, in offering this conceptualization of the ghostly present, marked by the possibility of active forgetting, I have wanted to suggest that desecularizing secularism, and the politics of complacency that accompany it, involves the task of dehistoricizing its history. This entails giving up certain historicist claims that secularism/secularists deploy to validate its identity. The task is made urgent by the contemporary crisis of secularism. As we have seen, the politics of complacency that govern secularist claims about the supposed secular state of our political modernity can hardly respond to this crisis. Such complacency cannot produce anything but a sense of despair when secularism becomes unable to reconcile its claims about the inviolability of its original history, its law, its truth, and its justice (traceable to an original temporal/spatial location—call it the constitution/first amendment) with post-original laws that supposedly threaten to violate, if they have not already violated, the equally original principle of the separation between religion and politics. Secularism cannot avoid the pitfalls of such despair so long as it continues to affirm

---

[34] Writing about majority directed violence against minorities in Sri Lanka, Sankaran Krishna argues: "we have to explain why, even as they help neighbors to escape or provide succor to victims, significant sections of the majority community feel the violence against minority community is, at a certain level, both understandable and necessary." See his *Postcolonial Insecurities: India, Sri Lanka, and the Question of Nationhood* (Minneapolis: University of Minnesota Press, 1999), 55 (emphasis added). Though there is some merit to this statement, the pursuit of the question of "why...", it seems to me, is no longer a worthwhile theoretical strategy.

the innocence of secularism's self-evident value and validity. Affirming innocence cannot pass for an argument. Affirming innocence cannot lead to taking political risks. For secularism to reckon with the crisis it faces, then, it will have to abandon the affirmation of the innocence of its history, of its appeal to law and right. This abandonment can be done only thorough a post-Nietzschean strategy of the active forgetting of its own history. My task has been to suggest that to think about the possibility of such active forgetting we need a Derridian strategy of the ghostly present that is out of joint with itself. Once secularism does the unthinkable task of rendering its own history unavailable for it to draw upon, to refer to, to remind itself of, it already finds itself in the ghostly present where its opponents themselves cannot appeal to their own historicist claims to counter those of the secularists.' Indeed, one might say that to be in the ghostly present is to have no recourse to history. Neither the secularists nor their opponents can appeal to history in the ghostly present because it is out of joint with itself. They cannot because in the disjunctured present they meet in active forgetting. It is in this present of forgetting that they may "live on," constructing their own arguments and claims in relation to its dying, ghostly moment. It is in that ghostly moment that they may, as Nietzsche would say, take walks in themselves. That, then, is, as Derrida would say, what "remains to come," be it post-secular justice or democracy.

Ananda Abeyesekere is Assistant Professor of Religion at Virginia Polytechnich University, Virginia. He is the author of <u>Colors of the Robe: Religion, Identity, and Difference</u> *(2004).*

DOMAINS RECOLLECTS, will be a regular feature.
In each issue, an important article, hitherto only available in Sri Lanka, will be republished, enabling international readers access to it.

We are honored to publish as our first recollection former ICES editor Regi Siriwardena's brilliant, yet largely unknown, critique of Edward Said's *Culture and Imperialism*. It was first given as a lecture at ICES in early 1993, and later published in the old ICES journal, *The Thatched Patio*, 6(3)1993: 27-41.

Said, the European Novel & Imperialism: A Critique

Regi Siriwardena[1]

My critique of Edward Said's new book *Culture and Imperialism*[2] will be directed essentially to its first two chapters, whose main concern is to argue that there is a close relation between imperialism and the European, and most particularly, the English novel. These two chapters are in fact the most substantial and original part of the book. Said's undertaking can be seen as, in some ways, a continuation and extension of his earlier book *Orientalism*[3], since both works seek to explore the significance of modes of representation as a source of power. In the book he is concerned to show that imperialism isn't sustained only by armies or policemen but also by the structures of acceptance induced through culture and especially for his purpose, through literature.

In his introduction to the new book, Said notes that what he had left out of *Orientalism* was "that response to Western dominance which culminated in the great movement of decolonization all across the Third World" (xii). The third chapter of *Culture and Imperialism* is headed 'Resistance and Opposition' as if to make up for that earlier lack. However, there is a curious dichotomy between material and method between the two parts of the book. In the first two chapters the general argument about the significance of culture in sustaining and securing consent to the imperialist enterprise is supported by interpretations of several novels, and also of one opera- Verdi's *Aida*. We expect, therefore, that in the third chapter Said will similarly exemplify his account

---

[1] This article first appeared in *The Thatched Patio* 6, no. 3 (1993): 27-41. Some of the citations have been modified and changed when necessary.
[2] Edward, Said. *Culture and Imperialism.* (New York: Vintage Books, 1994). [modified citation]
[3] Idem. *Orientalism: Western Conceptions of the Orient.* (London: Penguin, 1978). [new citation]

of the resistance of the colonised through readings of Third World texts by Creative artists. Instead, the texts he chooses for extended treatment in Chapter Three are five works of historical and socio-logical writing, and such references as there are to Third World poetry or fiction are extremely brief and perfunctory. It isn't my purpose to suggest that there are watertight compartments be-tween different fields of writing; but Said's method is unfortunate, because it may give the impression that Marquez, Rushdie, Wal-cott or Achebe don't deserve the kind of detailed treatment that Jane Austen, Kipling, Conrad or Camus get in the first part of the book. It's all the more odd that there is one poet who gets fuller treatment in the chapter on "Resistance and Opposition," and that isn't an Asian, African or Latin-American writer but W.B. Yeats, discussed here as a poet of Irish decolonisation. It's a strange choice because Yeats' relations with Irish nationalism on the one hand and the Anglo-Irish ruling class on the other were very ambivalent. It's not that Said is unaware of this fact, but to my mind it doesn't get clearly focussed in his discussion of the poetry. There are many things in this sub-chapter on Yeats that I should have liked to quarrel with, but I am leaving them out be-cause they are outside the scope of this paper. The fourth chapter is devoted to America's imperial role in the post-Cold War world as the last superpower and the heir to the Western empires of the past. I have no disagreement with Said's political position in this chapter, but he doesn't seem to me to say more than has been said already by other radical political writers.

So to get back to my real subject - Said, the European Novel and Imperialism. Said says early in his book: "I have delib-erately abstained from advancing a completely worked out theory of the connection between literature and culture on the one hand, and imperialism on the other. Instead, I hope the connections will emerge from their explicit places in the various texts" (14). He also says in his introduction, "My method is to focus as much as possible on individual works, to read them first as great products of the creative or interpretative imagination, and then to show them as part of the relationship between culture and empire" (xxii). Reading that last sentence, one may be inclined to raise a querying eyebrow. To read the works first as great literature *and then* to see them in their relationship with empire? Shouldn't these acts of reading and judgment, one may ask, be more integrated? If the involvement with empire in a novel matters at all, shouldn't the evidence be there in the very literary fabric of the work itself? Later in the book Said inveighs against the academic tendency to sanitize culture as a "realm of unchanging intellectual monuments, free from worldly affiliations," (13) or to see novels as "the product of lonely genius" or "manifestations of unconditioned creativity" (73). Although he says, "My principal aim is not to separate but to connect," (15) isn't Said, in defining his method as he does, making a kind of separation too? Of course, at first reading one treats that sentence as a carelessly imperfect formulation. But it turns out that the misgivings it arouses are justified, for there is, as I shall try to establish, a certain hiatus between Said's literary or aesthetic judgments and his political analysis.

For all Said's insistence that he is less concerned with theory than with demonstrating his conclusions from specific texts, he does have a theory of the novel and its relations with empire - and a pretty explicit one too. "The novel," he says, "is fundamentally tied to bourgeois society; in Charles Moraze's phrase, it accompanies, and is indeed a part of the conquest of Western society by what he calls *les bourgeois conquerants*. No less significantly, the novel is inaugurated in England *by Robinson Crusoe*, a work whose protagonist is the founder of a new world, which he rules and reclaims for Christianity and England (70). Said has been preceded by other theorists in characterising the novel as a bourgeois literary form; what he adds is the link with imperialism. In his words, "the novel, as a cultural artefact of bourgeois society, and imperialism are unthinkable without each other" (71).

Said's examination of the European novel is very English-centred; of the five novelists discussed in some detail in the first two chapters, four- Austen, Kipling, Conrad and Forster-are English. Said's defense of this selectivity is based partly on a belief in the literary supremacy of the English novel and partly on a historical view of the character of British imperialism. In his introduction Said says, "since narrative plays such a remarkable part in the imperial quest, it is therefore not surprising that France and (especially) England have an unbroken tradition of novel-writing, unparalleled elsewhere" (xxii). However, in the body of the book the claim for the uniqueness of the English novel is still more strongly asserted, even in comparison with France: "Britain...produced and sustained a novelistic institution with no real European competitor or equivalent" (71). And for Said the literary dominance of the English novel and the political dominance of British imperialism are not coincidental developments but essentially interconnected, because "imperialism and the novel fortified each other to such a degree that it is impossible to read one without in some way dealing with the other" (71).

Said also argues that British imperialism was unique in the degree of centrality it occupied in relation to national life. Of Russian imperialism he says: "Russia...acquired its imperial territories almost exclusively by adjacence. Unlike Britain or France, which jumped thousands of miles beyond their own borders to other continents, Russia moved to swallow whatever lands or peoples stood next to its borders, which in the process kept moving further east and south. But in the English and French cases, the sheer distance of attractive territories summoned the projection of far-flung interests" (10). However, in Said's view, even France offers no real parallel to the pervasive presence of imperialism in British society. "The reverses of policy, losses of colonies, insecurity of possession, and shifts in philosophy that France suffered during the Revolution and the Napoleonic era meant that its empire had a less secure identity and presence in French culture.... In the culture at large - until after the middle of the [19th] century - there is rarely that weighty, almost philosophical sense of imperial mission that one finds in Britain" (63).

I have been at pains to present this complex of ideas rather fully, and as far as possible in Said's own words, because I want to look at them critically. First, I wish to look at the view that the novel was the cultural product of the bourgeoisie. This is a proposition that has been much favoured by Marxist literary historians, but it was also advanced by a British scholar in a book published in 1957 that has been academically very influential - Ian Watt's *The Rise of the Novel: Studies in Defoe, Richardson and Fielding*[4] (though Watt said 'middle class' and not 'bourgeoisie'). And as long as one looks at the novel-form through the prism of the English novel, this view may seem unquestionable. Ian Watt's book, in spite of its title, turns out in fact to be about the rise of the English novel. Like Said, Watt claimed *Robinson Crusoe* as the first novel in English, one which is virtually a celebration of the new bourgeois hero, his adventurousness, his self-reliance, his conviction that Providence is with him, and his single-handed inauguration of what amounts to a colonial enterprise.

But does the notion that the novel was the creation of the bourgeoisie stand up when one goes beyond England? It is of course true that novels, as distinct from older European forms of narrative, were produced as printed books, and therefore required some elements of what has been called 'print capitalism,' the establishment of the printing press and the growth of the book market. But once these conditions had come into existence, the novel could flourish in societies where the bourgeoisie were not the dominant class such as 17th and 18th century France, and 19th century Russia. In the major French novels of the 17th and 18th centuries, such as Mme. de La Fayette's, *La Princesse de Cleves* and Choderlos de Laclos's *Les Liaisons Dangereuses,* the social milieu and the values are aristocratic and not bourgeois, as were the authors themselves. The very opening words of *La Princesse de Cleves* are 'magnificence and gallantry' - describing the atmosphere of the court of Henry II. The theme of the novel is the conflict between love and duty or honour in a highly elegant courtly society, outside of which the novel never moves. Laclos' novel is set in an aristocratic world seething with sexual intrigue, in which the conflict is between men and women in their struggle for sexual power. In 19th century Russia the novels of Pushkin, Lermontov, Gogol, Goncharov, and the early work of Turgenev, Tolstoy and Dostoevsky were produced in a society that had still not been emancipated from serfdom. And all these novelists came from the class that was known as *dvoryane* - that is nobility or

[4] Ian Watts. *The Rise of the Novel: Studies in Defoe, Richardson and Fielding.* (Berkeley: University of California Press: 1957). [modified citation]

gentry, and enjoyed legal rights and privileges by virtue of this fact. It is not till the last two decades of the 19th century that there was a major writer of Russian fiction who was not born into this class - that is Chekhov, whose family belonged to the petit-bourgeoisie.

The generalisation about the 'bourgeois' character of the novel is, therefore, an illegitimate extension from the English case. It's not that the novel is inherently a bourgeois literary form, but that in England, which was already a bourgeois society, the novel became a vehicle for bourgeois values. It's worth remarking that Ian Watt, in trying to establish that the novel is characterised by middle-class realism and in giving primacy to Defoe as the creator of the novel, says that "French fiction from *La Princesse de Cleves* to *Les Liaisons Dangereuses* stands outside the main tradition of the novel. For all its psychological penetration and literary skill, we feel it is too stylish to be authentic".[5] It's a circular process of reasoning; you first eliminate from the category of novels everything that doesn't fit the attributes you want to find in them, and then you define the novel in terms of what you have sieved out.

What of the supposed literary predominance of the English novel over its European rivals? It can reasonably be argued that the French novel has just as unbroken a tradition as the English (and even older if *Robinson Crusoe* is taken to be the first English novel), and one that is in no way inferior. There is in the Said of this book an unhappy mixture of the pamphleteer and the scholar, as I shall bring out more fully later,[6] but it already comes out in the way he slants his case about the novel and imperialism. Because he wants to demonstrate the interdependence between these two, which by his own account is less evident in the French case, he has to depreciate the French novel. Of course, the Russian novel was of later provenance than the English simply because printed literature itself emerged in Russia later than in Western

---

[5] Ibid., 30. [modified citation]

[6] In saying this I am not referring to the passion and anger that often manifest themselves in the book, as I see no reason why scholars should not feel these emotions. My point is that the scholar, even when moved in this way, should have scrupulous respect for the facts.

Europe. But, in the 19th century is the achievement of the Russian novel inferior to the English? Many English critics and novelists themselves have thought very differently. One may recall that the generation of young English novelists around the time of the First World War (Lawrence, Forster, Virginia Woolf) was fascinated by the Russian novel, to which they had been introduced by the translations of Constance Garnett, because they thought it superior to anything in their own language.

One observation of Said can serve as a reminder of how different the 19th century Russian novel was from the English. He writes:

> The novelistic hero and heroine exhibit the restlessness and energy characteristic of the enterprising bourgeois, and they are permitted adventures in which their experiences reveal to them the limits of what they can aspire to, where they can go, what they can become. Novels therefore end either with the death of a hero or heroine (Julien Sorel, Emma Bovary, Bezarov [sic], Jude the Obscure) who by virtue of overflowing energy does not fit into the orderly scheme of things, or with the protagonists' accession to stability (usually in the form of marriage or confirmed identity, as is the case with novels of Austen, Dickens, Thackeray, and George Eliot) (71).

Said doesn't seem to have thought it worth noting that in the first pattern of endings he distinguishes in the novel, all but one of the four he refers to are French or Russian, while the novels he mentions in the second group are those of English writers. The incorporation into society and achieved stability of the hero (usually through marriage, with property often in the background) is in fact the normal ending of the 19th century English novel. Hardy, the creator of Jude whom Said mentions in his first group is in this respect an exception, and he comes late in the century, when the order of Victorian society was being questioned by new intellectual currents. It's worth remarking that in *Wuthering Heights,* which in many ways is deviant from the mainstream Victorian novel, the tragic outcome of the relationship of Heathcliff and Catherine Earnshaw in the first half of the book is balanced by the achieved harmony of the younger pair, Hareton Earnshaw and Catherine Linton, in the second half. It's also noteworthy that on the one occasion when Dickens tried to break with the pattern of resolution through marriage -in the original ending of *Great Expectations* - he was persuaded by his friend Bulwer Lytton to conform to the established norm. But the most important point I want to make is that not a single major Russian novel of the 19th century resembles the English novel in this respect, nor would it be possible to fit *War and Peace* or any of the novels of Dostoevsky into either of the structural types distinguished by Said. If the 19th century English novel was directed towards the hero's successful incorporation into the stable order of bourgeois society, the Russian novel wasn't.

It seems to me, therefore, that Said's argument for basing a general case regarding culture and imperialism on the English novel is built on questionable literary foundations. I shall return later to the political contrasts he makes between British, French and Russian imperialisms, but now I want to look at one of his literary case-studies based on English texts. The case is that of Jane Austen's *Mansfield Park*. I must be honest and say that I haven't chosen it as the best piece of criticism in the book for he does much better with Conrad and Kipling. But I want to focus on the example of *Mansfield Park* because it brings out particularly sharply some of the problems raised by Said's critical method.

Said is perhaps the first critic of the novel to underline the fact that the affluence and gentility of the Bertram family at Mansfield Park is derived from a property in Antigua in the West Indies. Readers, if they take note of this fact at all, would generally treat it as a mechanism of the plot. It is Sir Thomas Bertram's absence in Antigua that permits the intrigues that go on round the projected domestic theatricals, thrown into confusion later by his unexpected return. But Said discovers in the Antiguan element a historical phenomenon that is an important part of the social reality that the novel presents:

> According to Austen we are to conclude that no matter
> how isolated and insulated the English place (e.g. Mans-

field Park), it requires overseas sustenance. Sir Thomas's property in the Caribbean would have had to be a sugar plantation maintained by slave labour (not abolished until the 1830s. These are not dead historical facts, but, as Austen evidently knew, evident historical realities (89).

Said's inference from the text that the comfortable world of Mansfield Park was sustained by slave labour will probably outrage some literary critics, but I think his point is incontrovertible and he is right to make it. The real question, however, is that once we have made this discovery, how does it affect our response to the novel? Said considers one possible reaction only to reject it. "Yes, Austen belonged to a slave-owning society, but do we therefore jettison her novels as so many trivial exercises in aesthetic frumpery? Not at all I would argue..." (96)

One can readily imagine exponents of vulgar Marxist literary criticism, so common in Sri Lanka, adopting just the position that Said rejects. It has often struck me that critics of this kind don't need even to read the novel, see the play or watch the film they are damning; they could as well work from a synopsis, because all that's necessary for them is to extract from the work a social message and then measure it as 'progressive' or 'reactionary.'

But what is Said's alternative? "Having read *Mansfield Park* as part of the structure of an expanding imperialist venture, one cannot simply restore it to the canon of 'great literary masterpieces' - to which it most certainly belongs- and leave it at that" (95). What Said wants to emphasise is the contradiction between Austen's civilized values and the reality of slavery which is part of that civilisation's economic underpinnings. "There is a paradox here in reading Jane Austen which I have been impressed by but can in no way resolve. All the evidence says that even the most routine aspects of holding slaves on a West Indian sugar plantation were cruel stuff. And everything we know about Austen and her values is at odds with the cruelty of slavery (96).

Although I don't share the position of the naive Marxist critics, I can't go along with Said either. In reading these passages I have quoted, there is a point at which I feel inclined to rub my eyes. This is the point at which he says — in a parenthesis, as if it

were self-evident- that *Mansfield Park* belongs "most certainly" to
the canon of "great literary masterpieces." Shouldn't a critic as
good as Said be less acquiescent about this canon? And nothing is
offered to justify that literary valuation of *Mansfield Park*, which
stands unrelated to the political critique that Said has just made
of it.

It can't be that Said has simply accepted inertly the conventional academic estimation of Jane Austen: he is too independent and perceptive a critic for that. No, I suggest that what he is
indulging in are the shock-tactics of the pamphleteer. He seems in
effect to be saying, 'Here is this great humane literary masterpiece,
and look at the skeleton in the cupboard, the worm in the apple
that it conceals — slavery!' The shock would be much diminished
if one were to say (as I would) that *Mansfield Park* isn't a great
novel at all but perhaps Austen's worst, with her most unpleasant
heroine, Fanny Price, a prudish and priggish Cinderella (Said himself calls her 'the neglected, demure and upright Wallflower').

But the question at issue concerns more than our opinion
of this one novel. The fact is that Austen's art, in spite of its feline
sharpness within its chosen bounds, is based on the exclusion of
any realities that would disturb her confidence in the order and
stability and fundamental rightness of her world. Fanny Price, the
poor relation, ends as the destined mistress of Mansfield Park.
Not because any criticism of the hierarchical class structure is implied, but because Fanny is in spirit a better embodiment and
guardian of the ideal values of the traditional order than her up-
per-class rival Mary Crawford. "Everything we know about Austen and her values," says Said, "is at odds with the cruelty of
slavery" (96). Is it? What matters is not whether she would have
approved of slavery if a direct question were put to her, but 'everything we know about Austen and her values' suggests that she
would have been quite happy to turn a blind eye to it. "Let other
pens dwell on guilt and misery. I quit such odious subjects as soon
as I can, impatient to restore everybody, not greatly in fault them-

selves, to tolerable comfort, and to have done with all the rest."[7] That is how the last chapter of *Mansfield Park* opens. If Austen could have been indifferent to so much 'guilt and misery' nearer home, taking a slave plantation for granted as the source of the order and civilisation she valued would hardly have been problematic to her.

Surely the great works of literature are those which, in some degree or other, question, disturb, challenge established certainties and not those which reinforce them. "A book," said Kafka, "should be the axe to break the frozen sea within us." I can't see how Said reconciles his valuation of Jane Austen with the terms in which he assesses Conrad. For what he values in *Heart of Darkness* and *Nostromo* is their critical insight into the processes of colonialism, the way in which they lay bare the pretensions and delusions of imperialism. But the contradictions that Said finds in Conrad are situated at a much deeper level than that in Austen. It lies in the fact that Conrad was incapable of seeing any potential human alternative in the colonised - the Africans, the Latin Americans or the American Indians - who are depicted as existing only to be enslaved, tyrannised over, manipulated. "He writes as a man whose Western view of the non-Western world is so ingrained as to blind him to other histories, other cultures, other aspirations. All Conrad can see is a world totally dominated by the Atlantic West in which every opposition to the West only confirms the West's wicked power." (xviii). And again: "As a creature of his time" writes Said, "Conrad could not grant the natives their freedom, despite his severe critique of the imperialism that enslaved them" (30).

Excellent as Said's discussion of Conrad is, I want now to dissent in some degree from that last sentence, with its partially exculpating phrase, 'as a creature of his time.' What it implies is that until the decolonising movements later in the twentieth cen-

---

[7] Jane Austen. *Mansfield Park*. (London: Penguin, 1994), 466. [new citation] There is, to be sure, a note of something close to playful self-mockery here. But the purpose of the seemingly self-critical irony (the deliberate flaunting of her fastidious distaste, 'such odious subjects') is to disarm potential criticism, so that there isn't real self-criticism here: the irony is defensive and serves a strategy of exclusion.

tury, a Western artist couldn't have been expected to see the colonised in their full humanity. But there was always resistance of
some kind to imperialism in the colonial world. I am not a be-
liever in 'unconditioned creativity', but Conrad's failure to achieve
the moral independence and courage to transcend the impasse in
which he found himself is as much a criticism of his own limitations as of the British imperialist milieu in which he lived and
wrote. No doubt the independence and courage required were of
a rare order. But that they weren't humanly impossible of attain-
ment is shown by the case of another novelist who was writing
around the same time that Conrad was producing *Nostromo* and
Heart of Darkness. As a prelude to this comparison, I need to go
back to the contrasts that Said makes between the British, French
and Russian empires.

You will recall my summary of Said's argument that the
empire was less central to French and Russian national life than
to the British. This seems the suitable place at which to observe
that there is a certain gap between Said's' large generalisations
and the actual literary evidence he is able to produce. You can't
understand the novel, he says, without understanding imperialism,
but even in the British case on which he specially relies, how
much is there in the book to support this challenging statement?
Said is able to show quite convincingly that even 19th century
British thinkers and writers who were critics of their society, like
Carlyle, Ruskin, Arnold, and Dickens were supportive of the imperialist enterprise; but how much evidence is there of this in the
novel? After Crusoe what? Said is able to demonstrate the sub-
merged presence of colonialism in Austen, Dickens, Thackeray,
but the fact remains that for writers who treated the colonial experience frontally he has to fall back on the familiar trinity whom
every chronicler of the colonial novel has written about: Kipling,
Conrad, Forster. At the height of empire the theme was relegated
to a sub-literary genre cultivated by the likes of Rider Haggard,
Ballantyne and Henty, belonging in fact to the province of boys'
fiction. That being so, what meaning are we to give to Said's,
proposition that you can't understand the novel without understanding imperialism? As far as I can see, the only way in which
one can support it in the British case is to say that imperialism

was, by and large, a significant absence in the 18th and 19th century English novel, which of course tells us a great deal about the culture of the literati.[8] But one could construct other propositions for which the evidence can be found on nearly every page of the classic English novels - for instance, 'You can't understand the English novel without understanding the subordination of women', or 'you can't understand the English novel without understanding the hierarchical class character of English society.' What justifies privileging imperialism as the single overarching reality to which the novel has to be related?

It was the distinction of Conrad and Kipling to have brought the colonial theme into the established canon of English literature. Discussing Kipling and Conrad in relation to the genre of adventure-imperialism, Said says that their work, while belonging to it, claims "serious aesthetic and critical attention" (155). There are two points I want to make about this. One is that the recognition of their work in that light was posthumous - in fact, post-Second World War.[9] The other is that their writing was made possible by what were in their time exceptional circumstances. Conrad was a Pole by birth who had served in the British Merchant Marine, and Kipling had been born in India and therefore chose to go back there as a young journalist. Imperialism, however significant for British society, became more than marginal to English literature only after the empire had been lost in the aftermath of the Second World War.[10]

---

[8] Said recognizes this in his own way when he says that in the 19th century empire was a "marginally visible presence in fiction" (63). I find this admission difficult to reconcile with the sweeping claims made elsewhere in the book for its overriding importance for English fiction.

[9] The great valuation today of Conrad as one of the great English novelists is principally due to F.R. Leavis's, *The Great Tradition: George Eliot, Henry James, Joseph Conrad* (1948; reprint, New York: New York University Press, 1964), [modified citation], published twenty-five years after Conrad's death. Serious critical attention to Kipling is even more recent.

[10] The popularity in Britain not only of novels such as those of Paul Scott, J.G. Farrell and Timothy Mo but also of TV serials about the British Raj testifies to the retrospective interest today in empire. Another relevant phenomenon is the academic institution of the study of colonial fiction (which wasn't an academic subject when the empire was intact). Culturally, therefore, the empire has been more alive since it died.

I now want to question Said's view that empire was less central to Russian life than to British (he may be right about the French case). Of course, there was a difference between British expansion overseas and Russian expansion into neighbouring territories. This was a consequence both of the late and weak development of Russian sea-power and of the fact that Russia had a vast continental hinterland, inhabited mainly by tribal peoples, into which it could expand. But I don't see that this difference between sea-based and land-based empires made a fundamental difference to the importance of empire for each nation. On the other hand, as far as the literary consciousness of empire was concerned, I should like to offer a contrary argument. Most 19th Century English novelists, even if they had wanted to treat imperialism imaginatively, would hardly have had the experience to do so. Contrast this with the Russian situation. On the one hand Russian literature was produced in the 19th century mainly by members of an aristocratic class, who often took to military service as part of their way of life and served on the frontier; on the other hand, the colonised territories were also places to which dissenting intellectuals were sent as exiles or political prisoners. In contrast with the English case, therefore, we have in 19th century Russia no less than four major writers who saw life on the frontier at first hand - Pushkin as an exile, Tolstoy as an army officer, Lermontov as both, and Dostoevsky as a convict and as a conscript serving a penal term in the army. Four who include the greatest Russian poet of the century and the two greatest novelists.

However, precisely because 19th century Russian literature was written by an aristocratic intelligentsia, it doesn't share the sense of empire as the source of prosperity and the bourgeois advancement of the hero that Said finds in the English novel. Said points out, for instance, that Pip in *Great Expectations,* having lost one fortune made in Australia by Magwitch has, by the end of the novel, achieved another, though more modest one, through Herbert's trading business with the colonies- sugar, tobacco and rum from the West Indies and elephant tusks from Ceylon. This is hardly what one would expect to find meaningful to the heroes of the Russian fiction of empire; and one doesn't. Instead, in Pushkin's early narrative poem "A Prisoner in the Caucasus" and in the first chapter of Lermontov's novel *A Hero of our Time,* the frontier is the exotic site of military adventures and romantic encounters. In these two stories the conquest, emotional or sexual, of a native woman by a man of the colonizing race presents a transformation in fantasy of the relationship of subjection and domination between conquerors and conquered. The woman gives her love generously, devotedly (which is what the colonizer would desire ideally of all the colonized), but since love between the sexes transgresses the racial barriers, she has in the end to die. One may think of the parallel in Kipling's story 'Without Benefit of Clergy.' In Pushkin's poem the love is one-sided, entirely on the woman's part; she finally helps the Russian, who has been taken prisoner by her people, to escape, and then kills herself. In Lermontov's novel the Russian officer Pechorin kidnaps Bela, wins her love, then tires of her as he tires of everything. She is finally killed by a young man of her own race who had desired her. In both stories the 'wild' life of the frontier is seen as more elemental and more natural than the civilized, but this in no-way negates the imperial mission. It is quite striking, in fact, in Pushkin's poem that when the escaped captive finds his way back to the Russian camp, the return to normality is marked by his sight of the Russian bayonets shining through the mist; and this leads into the epilogue which celebrates quite unequivocally the triumph of Russian arms in the Caucasus. But let me now present in contrast the very different treatment of imperialism in the later work of Tolstoy.

Said expresses in more than one place in his book the need to transcend the cultural exclusiveness of many Third World nationalisms and "the hostility between Western and non-Western cultures that leads to crises" (19). Given that aspiration, it is necessary that we should not only identify and expose the racist assumptions - open or concealed - in many manifestations of Western culture but that we should also recognise the rare alternative voices within the Western tradition itself. They include Jonathan Swift and Mark Twain, but in the Western novel in the heyday of empire the supreme dissenting voice, supreme both in moral integrity and in creative power - is that of Tolstoy. I want to conclude with an account of three of his works which have a bearing on the imperial theme. I hope my account will bring out what has been excluded in Said's generalisations about the European novel and imperialism. It should surely be of relevance that the writer whom many readers would consider the greatest of Western novelists, was also the most searching and eloquent critic of imperialism through the medium of the novelist's art.

Tolstoy wrote his last novel *Hadji Murat*[11], and his short story "After the Ball"[12] in the same opening decade of the twentieth century in which Conrad published *Heart of Darkness* and *Nostromo*, the short story "Does a Man Need Much Land?"[13] was written even earlier in 1886. *Hadji Murat* was written in the teeth not only of Tolstoy's renunciation of art in his latter years but also of his pacifism. It takes as its hero a historical character, a Caucasian fighter against the Russians. At the beginning of the novel the narrator is reminded of him by the sight of a thistle in a ploughed field, which, half-crushed and mutilated, is still struggling for life; and that thistle becomes the image of Hadji Murat's courage, spirit and inexhaustible physical vitality. Hadji Murat, however, is a tragic figure: having fallen out with Shamil, the political and religious leader of the Chechens, he deserts to the Russians. The local commander, Vorontsov, receives him well and wants to use him to pacify the Chechens. The strategy, however, is doomed to failure because the cold, ruthless and stupid despot Nicholas I wants to crush Chechen resistance by force.

There is no parallel in any earlier Western novel to the representation of imperialist violence in the middle chapters of *Hadji Murat*. The technique used is almost cinematic. First, we sit in on the conference between Nicholas and his Minister of War;

---

[11] The three Tolstoy stories that Siriwardena refers to are his own direct translations from Russian versions and are not referenced in the original version of the paper. Hence, we have only been able to cite the stories in general and have not traced the pages of some quotations. Leo Tolstoy. *Hadji Murat*. (Hesperus Press: London, 2003).

[12] Idem. *The Penguin Book of Russian Short Stories*, ed. David Richards (London: Penguin Books, 1981).

[13] It is usually translated as "how Much Land Does a Man Need?" but I see no reason not to keep the original Russian title. Idem. *How Much Land Does a Man Need? And Other Stories*. (London: Penguin, 1993).

then Tolstoy cuts to a Russian detachment raiding a defenceless Chechen village in pursuance of Nicholas's decision. This attack is seen through the eyes of Butler, a young Russian officer, experiencing all the tension and rapture of what he regards as the poetry of war. Then, in a complete reversal of angle, we are shifted to the Chechen village with men, women and children among the ruins of their smashed and burnt houses and their slain, divided between mourning and hatred and repulsion against the Russians, the desire to exterminate them "like rats, poisonous spiders or wolves." It's hardly surprising that the Tsarist censors refused to allow the greater part of these chapters when the novel was first published after Tolstoy's death.

Hadji Murat attempts to escape from the Russian camp because Shamil has branded him a traitor and has threatened terrible reprisals against his family. He wants to take to the mountains and continue the struggle against Shamil. His followers, who had been personally loyal to him, are glad of the chance to fight the Russians again: this indicates that they must have always thought him to be in error in joining the Russians. (Meanwhile, back at home, even Hadji Murat's own son, threatened with blinding by Shamil as a punishment for his father's treason, doesn't share the latter's hostility to Shamil.) The novel ends with Hadji Murat's last stand against the Russian pursuers, hopelessly outnumbered and encircled. He is killed, his body hacked to pieces, and his head cut off and borne back as a trophy. When it is triumphantly displayed, Butler's mistress, Marya Dmitrievna, who had come to admire Hadji Murat when he was in the camp, turns away from her lover in anger and disgust: "You are cutthroats all."

In "After the Ball" the narrator, Ivan Vasilyevich goes out into the fields one morning, deliriously happy after dancing the whole night with the girl with whom he was in love. By chance he sees a Tatar conscript, who had tried to escape, being made to run the gauntlet of a company of soldiers. His back is a bleeding mass of flesh, and watching this brutal scene impassively is the colonel, in whom the narrator recognises the girl's father. This experience changes his whole life. He can never bring himself now to enter the army, as he had hoped. It's the end also of his love, because when he meets his girlfriend and she smiles her enchanting smile, he thinks of the expression with which her father had watched the flogging of the Tatar.

In *Hadji Murat* and 'After the Ball' the moral judgment on imperialism is very clear; in "Does a Man Need Much Land?" it's more oblique but perhaps even more powerful. Tolstoy is writing here at the height of his artistic powers, using a form that has the simplicity of a folk-tale but is yet enormously suggestive.[14] James Joyce once called it "the greatest story that the literature of the world knows."[15] It may be said that Tolstoy's desire in his latter years to write in such a way as to influence morally as large a public of ordinary readers as possible has borne fruit in the language and form of "Does A Man Need Much Land?"; the stripping away of any stylistic or formal excrescences does result in an art of great purity and power. Countess Tolstoy, writing to her husband about the ovation given to the story by an audience mainly of students who heard it publicly read at Moscow University in April 1886, described the general impression regarding the story: "that the style is remarkably austere, concentrated, not a superfluous word, everything sure, precise, like a musical chord; much content, few words, and wholly satisfying."[16]

The story concerns a Russian, Pahom, who begins life as an ordinary peasant, but becomes gradually richer and richer by accumulating more and more land. However, he is never satisfied and always looks for more land. One day a merchant tells him that in the country of the Bashkirs there is any amount of fertile land to be got cheap. Pahom goes to the country of the Bashkirs and finds a nomad pastoral people, living in wagons, who don't plough the land, the open endless steppe. Pahom is told by their

---

[14] An editorial note in L.N. Tolstoy, *Sobranie Sochinenly v dvadtsati dvuh tomah* 19 (1982): 532-533, states that the motif of a man staking a claim to a plot of land by walking or running around it, only to fall dead, is found in some Ukranian folk-tales.

[15] In a letter to his daughter Lucia on 27 April 1935, Stuart Gilbert, ed., *Letters of James Joyce* Vol. 1 (London: Faber and Faber, 1957), 364. It is interesting that Joyce, who in 1935 was engaged on the labyrinthine art of Finnegans Wake, should have responded so warmly to the simple elemental quality of storytelling in "Does a Man Need Much Land?"

[16] Tolstoy. *Sobranie Sochinenly v dvadtsati dvuh tomah* 19: 533.

chief, after a long consultation among the Bashkirs, that they don't sell land by its area but by the day. He will be taken out at dawn to a place where they will set a mark; beginning there, he can walk in any direction, tracing as large a circle as he pleases, and provided he returns to the starting-point by sunset, all the land within the circle he has traced will be his. Pahom begins walking in the morning but is constantly tempted by his greed to enlarge his circle, and by the time he begins returning, it is late; the sun sinks lower and lower in the sky. Ultimately he desperately begins running back, with his mouth parched and his heart pounding; he finally makes it to the starting-point as the sun is sinking below the horizon, but collapses. Pahom's servant tries to revive him, but he is dead. The servant digs a grave and buries him. The question in the title is answered. Six feet of earth, that's all the land Pahom needed.

"Does a Man Need Much Land?" in its structure resembles some folk-tales about people who come to grief because they are never satisfied (Like *The Fisherman's Wife*), and it's usually read as a parable of individual greed. But the story acquires an altogether new dimension from the fact that its denouement is in the country of the Bashkirs, in the continental hinterland which was Russia's field of imperial expansion. When Pahom comes there looking for land, he comes as a coloniser. It's quite clear in the story that the idea of private property in land is alien to the Bashkirs: they do not even plough the land, let alone own it. The method by which Pahom is supposed to mark out his land is obviously quite fantastic. It might be supposed to be in keeping with the non-realistic, folk-tale atmosphere of the story. But, given the encounter between the Russian alien and the nomad people, it acquires another meaning. From the long consultations among the Bashkirs before the offer is made, it seems evident that they are trapping him. They have sensed his greed and they have devised a stratagem by which they can use it to destroy him.

The motive force of the whole story is the drive for land, territory - the main goal of colonial expansion. "Does a Man Need Much Land?" becomes therefore a parable not only about individual greed but also about colonial expansion. The Bashkirs are in the position of many colonised peoples who, unable to resist with force, the superior power of the coloniser have to resort to devious strategies of resistance. And doesn't Pahom's end, imagined by Tolstoy a century ago, foreshadow the self-destructive course of colonialism- of the empires we have seen collapsing and those we may still see collapse because they have tried to possess too much?

Regi Siriwardena edited Thatched Patio, later re-named Nethra, which he called 'a non specialist journal for lively minds' until 2003. A novelist, playwright and poet, he is one of Sri Lanka's foremost literary critics.

"...They are finely nuanced, sensitive, controlled and evocative. Each carefully chosen detail, each fragment of conversation call up a world, a time and a place that is totally familiar to the Sri Lankan reader. Yet, one cannot but see it anew. The angle of refraction has shifted ever so slightly. It is as if the writer positions himself 'at the water's edge' between sea and shore and this very marginality produces new insights into the familiar. The controlled writing, the carefully understated descriptions of people and actions weave a moving commentary on life as lived.... The spare style where every detail sets up a chain of resonance gives emotional power to the whole so that one is left thinking about the stories long after one has closed the book."

— *Ranjini Obeyesekere*

"...certainly a winner."
—*www.desijournal.com*

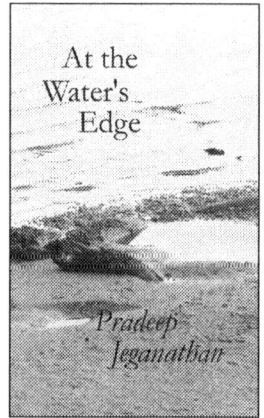

Pradeep Jeganathan's
At The Water's Edge

New York,
South Focus Press
ISBN:
0974883905

"This is an excellent beginning by a new author and the possibility of an authentic new voice from Sri Lanka is an exciting one."

—*Asian Review of Books*

"Pradeep Jeganathan has certainly mastered the art of the short story."

—*www. sangam.org*

www.ingramcontent.com/pod-product-compliance
Lightning Source LLC
Chambersburg PA
CBHW031210270326
41931CB00006B/494